A GARDEN OF ROSES

Published in association with the
Royal Horticultural Society

A GARDEN OF ROSES

Watercolours by Alfred Parsons, RA

Commentary by
Graham Stuart Thomas, OBE, VMH, DHM, VMM
Gardens Consultant to the National Trust

Biographical note by Professor Bryan Brooke

Salem House

Other books by Graham Stuart Thomas

The Old Shrub Roses
Colour in the Winter Garden
Shrub Roses of Today
Climbing Roses Old and New
Plants for Ground-Cover
Perennial Garden Plants
Gardens of the National Trust
Three Gardens
Trees in the Landscape
The Art of Planting

First published in the United States by
Salem House Publishers, 1987, 462 Boston Street,
Topsfield, MA 01983

The pictures on page 13 are reproduced by kind
permission of RJ Berkeley, Esq.

Associate editor: Russell Ash
Designed by Nick Hand

Library of Congress Cataloging-in-Publication Data

Thomas, Graham Stuart
A garden of roses.
Includes index.
1. Roses – History
2. Roses – Pictorial works.
3. Botanical illustration – England.
4. Watercolor painting, English.
I. Title.

SB 411.45.T46 1987   635.9′33372   86-33836
ISBN 0-88162-248-6

Typeset in Bodoni Old Face by Characters, Bristol
Colour separation by Rapier Press, London.
Printed in Italy by Arnoldo Mondadori

CONTENTS

PUBLISHER'S NOTE

In the early years of this century, Ellen Ann Willmott, a wealthy English gardening enthusiast, commissioned the painter, Alfred Parsons, RA, to record her roses for posterity. His painstaking work over several years resulted in 132 meticulously detailed watercolours, but his magnificent achievement was virtually unrecognised as a result of the inadequacies of the book in which they were reproduced, *The Genus Rosa*. The reproduction of the pictures was unsatisfactory and the text inaccurate, while the outbreak of the First World War finally halted any chances of the book's commercial success.

After Miss Willmott's death, the paintings passed, by way of the Cory Bequest, into the keeping of the Lindley Library at the Royal Horticultural Society in London, in association with which *A Garden of Roses* is published. The plates are reproduced from Parsons' original watercolours in order to achieve the fidelity that was intended but never achieved in *The Genus Rosa*.

In *A Garden of Roses*, the distinguished authority on roses, Graham Stuart Thomas, has chosen and described 70 of Alfred Parsons' finest pictures for *The Genus Rosa*. He introduces these with a survey of the history of rose cultivation and the background to Miss Willmott's ambitious project. Professor Bryan Brooke, a great-nephew of Alfred Parsons, presents a rare modern appraisal of this much neglected but important painter and his involvement with the ill-fated *The Genus Rosa*.

Who would look dangerously up at Planets that might safely look down on plants?

*Gerard's **Herball**, 1597*

The wonder of the world, the beauty and the power, the shapes of things, their colours, lights and shades; these I saw. Look ye also while life lasts.

*From **The Little Grey Men** by "BB", 1942*

A GARDEN OF ROSES

GRAHAM STUART THOMAS OBE VMH DHM VMM
Gardens Consultant to the National Trust

*Would Jove appoint some flowers to reign
In matchless beauty on the plain,
The Rose (mankind will all agree),
The Rose the Queen of Flowers should be.*

Sappho, Greek poetess, born c.600 BC

THE DERIVATION OF OUR GARDEN ROSES

It has taken well nigh two centuries to bring our modern roses, the Hybrid Teas and Floribundas and large-flowered climbers, to their present state of perfection. Through various records we have the story more or less complete, at least from just prior to 1800 to the present day. What had happened before that date and indeed in prehistoric times is supposition, though we have fairly clear pointers. I do not propose to trace all the evidence here – it would fill another book – but I want to set down the sequence of events since 1800 and to relate them to the work and writings of certain people who have done much to unravel the story.

First, however, we must visualize the extent of the genus and the status of the main species in our review. There are about 150 species extant, all natives of the Northern Hemisphere, in a complete band from east to west, from as far north as Kamtchatka, Siberia and Canada and as far south as Burma, Abyssinia and the southernmost of the United States of America. They vary from little suckering bushes a foot or two in height, to gigantic climbers of some 18m (60ft).

Although there have been hybrids made between many species, only a mere handful of species show to any marked degree their influence in developing the popular hybrids of today. They can be limited to three species from the Far East, and five species from the cradle of our civilization, in the eastern Mediterranean. Derived from two of the Far Eastern species were four hybrids of very ancient lineage; through various paths they reached Europe at the turn of the eighteenth century. The two parental Eastern species were *Rosa chinensis*, the China rose, and *R. gigantea*, the Tea rose; their hybrids became known in Europe as 'Parsons' Pink', 'Slater's Crimson', 'Hume's Blush' and 'Parks' Yellow'. They brought with them the valuable asset of repeatedly flowering through the growing season. No rose of true rich crimson had been seen by European gardeners until their arrival, for the so-called Red Rose

of Lancaster was merely a full, dark pink and not a full, dark crimson. From the China rose all the crimson roses of the last two centuries have been derived. We have no means of being certain which of the introductions became the ancestor of our red rose hybrids, especially as Dr Hurst recorded having seen what was to all intents and purposes a single-flowered, fertile plant, a graceful short climber at the Roseraie de l'Haÿ, near Paris, prior to 1914.

During the nineteenth century these roses became hybridized with the established roses of Europe, probably an equally ancient group. It is believed that these were descended from *R. gallica*, the French rose, *R. moschata*, the Musk rose, *R. phoenicea*, the Phoenician rose, and at a later date, a form of the Dog rose *R. canina*. Their intermarrying had given rise to groups known as Gallica, Damask, Centifolia and Alba. The hybrids arose at first by chance but later by intent when such skills became understood. They were later joined by hybrids of *R. multiflora* from Japan and *R. foetida* from the Middle East, the so-called Austrian Brier. This, then, is the basic story of the development of our garden roses which is, little by little, revealed in the descriptions of the roses recorded in colour in this book.

Collecting the old roses

The present enthusiasm for roses throughout much of the world was in a great way started by the Empress Joséphine, wife of Napoleon Bonaparte, who in 1799 went to live in the château of La Malmaison, not far from Paris. Born Marie-Josèphe-Rose Tascher de la Pagerie, her maiden name is immortalized in the genus *Lapageria*, closely related to the lilies, and her château by the famous, large, fragrant Malmaison carnations and the rose 'Souvenir de la Malmaison'. This was named long after her death by the Grand Duke of Russia in memory of her and her garden.

We are very fortunate that roses were favourites of Joséphine. She collected species and hybrids from Europe and countries abroad, and it is recorded that though Britain and France were at war, parcels of roses addressed to Malmaison were given safe conduct to French ports by our ships. Her garden contained many plants other than roses, but over 150 of these were superbly painted by the Belgian Pierre Joseph Redouté in *Les Roses*, between 1817 and 1824, with descriptions by C. A. Thory. Thus we have a record, which we must believe to be fairly complete, of the roses of the old European groups just as they were becoming hybridized with the Far Eastern roses. The beautiful paintings have been a source of admiration and inspiration ever since and the three magnificent volumes fetch many thousands of pounds when, occasionally, they come on the market. Fortunately sets of exact facsimiles were produced in Belgium in 1978, largely through the interest of Robert and Jelena de Belder, from a magnificent copy of the original, signed by Redouté, and which had previously been owned by Miss Ellen Ann Willmott. They are thus available to today's enthusiasts, without having recourse to museums and libraries. A valuable fourth volume, master-minded by Gordon D. Rowley, was added, bringing nomenclature up to date.

During the nineteenth century enormous strides were made in all branches of horticulture; flowering shrubs (including roses) began to be appreciated; famous nurseries specializing in roses came into prominence, such as Thomas Rivers of Sawbridgeworth, and William Paul & Sons of Cheshunt, both in Hertfordshire; in 1876 the (Royal) National Rose Society was formed; and William Robinson and Gertrude Jekyll sought to reinstate in gardens roses grown at Malmaison in opposition to the growing of roses for shows, which was the initial preoccupation of the Rose Society. This was in line with the several other British societies which specialized in single genera. During the century the hybridizing of the China roses with the Europeans gave rise first to the Bourbon roses, which perpetuated the mainly pink colouring of the Europeans coupled with the repeat-flowering of the Chinese; second to the pale yellow and coppery Tea-Noisette climbing roses; then to the Hybrid Perpetuals which first showed us the dark crimson inherent in the Chinese hybrids; and thence on to the Hybrid Teas. The prototype of this group is generally looked upon as 'La France' of 1867. Towards the end of the century new rambler roses were derived from *R. multiflora* from Japan. Hitherto all garden roses had been of soft colouring, from white, pink and crimson to purple and maroon, and from cream and pale yellow to coppery salmon.

By 1906 some 11,000 names of roses were recorded by Léon Simon and Pierre Cochet in their *Nomenclature de tous les Noms de Roses*. At about this time two important things happened. Monsieur Pernet-Ducher of Lyon succeeded in crossing the Persian Yellow rose with a Hybrid Perpetual, opening the door to the flood of vibrant flame and orange tints with which we are familiar today; and Miss Willmott, on the crest of her own prosperity and the Edwardian days of luxury (for the few), decided to create her own great book of roses. She commissioned the noted artist, Alfred Parsons, RA, to record the roses she had collected in her three gardens; at Great Warley, Essex; Tresserve, near Menton, and Boccanegra, near Ventimiglia. Her work appeared in parts from 1910 to 1914.

It will be noted that Miss Willmott was not interested in the multitudinous new hybrids, that were the principal preoccupation of the new specialist rose nurseries and even of the National Rose Society, but rather in the wild species and also the old garden forms and hybrids from Europe and China. But what with the First World War and the difficulties attendant upon the restoration of peace, little progress was made in reassessing the garden value of these splendid shrubs and climbers until Edward A. Bunyard, owner of a long-established nursery at Maidstone, Kent, produced his book *Old Garden Roses* in 1936. This was as enlightened a work as could be expected from an erudite and enthusiastic nurseryman and although he was unable to take advantage of Dr. C. C. Hurst's work on genetics, his book did much to awaken gardeners to the fast-disappearing names of many nineteenth-century varieties – and, indeed, did much to conserve the fast-disappearing plants. Further interruptions came with the Second World War and the premature death of Bunyard; and with the sale of the Bunyard roses and also those of Daisy Hill Nursery, Newry, County Down. The wholesale nursery of T. Hilling & Company of Woking, Surrey (the firm I was then working for), purchased all it could and also took over a big collection of other old roses, together with most species then in cultivation, listed by George Beckwith & Sons of the Hoddesdon nursery, Hertfordshire. Their catalogue was written by Arthur Osborn, Curator of Kew. These roses were planted and left to look after themselves until after the war. They survived the years of neglect.

As may be read in my book *The Old Shrub Roses*, first published in 1955, certain enthusiasts had preserved many other old garden roses for posterity and generously contributed these to our collection. This was catalogued in a descriptive list entitled *Roses as Flowering Shrubs*. After twenty-five years with T. Hilling & Company I left to become manager of Sunningdale Nurseries, Surrey, and took my rose collection with me, augmenting it all the time. Here was published *The Manual of Shrub Roses* in 1964. To my roses were added several which James Russell had collected at Sunningdale. Varieties continued to flow in from botanic gardens in the United States and two nurseries, Bobbink & Atkins of Rutherford, New Jersey, and Will Tillotson's nursery of Watsonville, California. They came, too, from growers and nurserymen in Denmark, Holland, Germany, France and Switzerland. Considerable numbers were obtained from the Roseraie de l'Haÿ and Bagatelle, near Paris, and from the East German national rose garden at Sangerhausen; unfortunately these three old national collections proved to be extremely unreliable in regard to nomenclature. Having acquired an extensive library of rose books of all ages, the work in checking was thorough and we listed very few roses without authentic names. Two in particular continue to baffle me; they are those we know as 'Empress Joséphine' and 'Fantin-Latour'. There is no record of a rose of either name in old books.

During these many years of searching for forgotten garden treasures, the species were to be found at Kew and also in the nursery of Hillier & Sons, Winchester. The latter collection which was once so all-embracing, has, sadly, now been curtailed.

The time came for me to leave Sunningdale Nurseries; fortunately the Royal National Rose Society at St Albans, Hertfordshire, was ready to devote part of its new grounds to the older and newer Shrub roses, and my collection was duplicated there. My time was much taken up with the National Trust, and a year or two later a walled garden at Mottisfont Abbey, Romsey, Hampshire, became vacant and the entire collection of old garden roses has thus found a permanent resting place. A further walled garden there was vacated in 1984 and many more varieties were obtained from Sangerhausen, which again needed considerable examination and sorting, and were planted in the spring of 1986. Meanwhile a similar great collection has been built up at Castle Howard, York, by James Russell and there are happily two nurseries offering a vast number of cultivars – David Austin Roses of Albrighton, Wolverhampton, and Peter Beales Roses of Attleborough, Norfolk.

But it would be of little use offering these roses for sale if they had not been taken to heart by the gardening public. What began with a trickle of admirers has now become a flood, with Old Rose groups in many countries. Old varieties continue to be found and authenticated. It seems that these heirlooms of the past are now safely restored to their rightful place. They have their admirers and their detractors, but all agree that there is nothing else like them in horticulture.

The work of scientists among roses
The growing of plants was undoubtedly started so that the housewife could have herbs at hand instead of roaming the countryside in search of supplies. The term "herb" was used to cover plants which were grown for cooking or for their supposed curative properties. The cult of herbs still survives and prospers. But by degrees certain plants were grown for their beauty, their affinities were studied, and the science of botany was born. As the centuries passed, plants were used to create desired aesthetic effects and in this way the art, as opposed to the craft, of gardening first began.

The earliest botany books were very much devoted to catalogues of culinary and medicinal plants, but later much skill and interest was given to the descriptions of ornamental plants. Towards the end of the

eighteenth century several important books on roses appeared, including the often-cited works of Johannes Herrmann and Mary Lawrance; the early nineteenth century saw many more published, including C. A. Thory's text in P. J. Redouté's three magnificent volumes. Ellen Willmott, with the help of J. G. Baker, often referred to these books and their findings in her two big volumes of *The Genus Rosa*.

Until the nineteenth century botanists had been content simply to describe roses as they saw them, to the best of their ability. Botany is not an exact science, and even today it leaves open the possibility of inaccurate descriptions. The early botanists had no real means of knowing whether they were looking at a good representation of a wild species or a garden hybrid, apart from the frequently double flowers of the latter. Such difficulties as these, coupled with the fact that a botanist in one country perhaps did not know of the work of a fellow botanist elsewhere, often caused considerable confusion in nomenclature. This explains why certain changes in nomenclature are imperative from time to time: closer examination of the records of the past may reveal ambiguities of detail, and further knowledge and research may enable a new concept of a species to be reached. Thus several of the names used in this volume are different from those used by Baker and Willmott.

When geneticists began to examine botanical findings of the past, further facts came to light that often clarified the status of a plant as a hybrid or a species in its own right. It is very much to the credit of Dr C. C. Hurst that great advances were made in the study of the parentage of roses. He founded in 1909 the Burbage Experiment Station for Genetics in Leicestershire, and among other genera of plants and animals he studied *Rosa*. Unfortunately his studies were interrupted by the First World War. Later he went up to Cambridge to work on the cytology of roses and in 1922, in collaboration with Mabel S. G. Breeze, he produced his "Notes on the Origin of the Moss Rose". War again, in 1939, interrupted his work, but much had been done and in 1941 his more exhaustive and comprehensive survey of roses appeared, entitled "Notes on the Origin and Evolution of Our Garden Roses". These were both published in the *Journal of the Royal Horticultural Society* for the years stated. It was in 1926-9 that I first came across him; as a student at the University Botanic Garden, Cambridge, I used on some occasions to attend to the cultivation of many of his experimental seedlings and it so happened that he and I both attended an extramural course of lectures on "Plant Life through the Ages" by Professor A. C. Seward. It was this earlier association with him that gave me added interest when his second lot of notes appeared. A whole new world of roses was revealed and it was from then that roses became of special interest to me. I was fascinated as the involved story of the parentage unfolded. Dr Hurst's two papers were republished by most kind permission of his widow in my first book, *The Old Shrub Roses,* in 1955.

The John Innes Horticultural Institute was originally stationed at Merton, Surrey; on its transference to Bayfordbury, Hertfordshire, more space was available. Here, Ann Wylie began her work on *Rosa,* which closely followed Hurst's; she checked and rechecked his notes and the cytology of the species and garden hybrids and recorded her findings in *Endeavour,* October 1955, No. 56, under the title of "The History of Garden Roses". Her work was in great part followed by that of the Keeper of Collections, Gordon D. Rowley, who was good enough to provide scientific background and charts to each of my three rose books. They both brought able brains to bear on the subject and it is good to mention that they found that except in a very few instances Hurst was right in his findings; moreover, they were able to add to our knowledge in various ways. The studies came to an untimely end when the Horticultural Institute became simply the John Innes Institution; Rowley left in 1961 and took up a lectureship in botany at Reading University but for several years was a splendid help to me on many aspects of the rose.

Many books have been written on roses since those days but little scientific knowledge was added until the appearance of the eighth edition of *Trees and Shrubs Hardy in the British Isles* by W. J. Bean. Desmond Clark, with whom I had the honour of being associated in the revision of the cultivars of the genus, has added enormously to our knowledge through his careful investigations. Volume IV should be in the hands of all rose enthusiasts.

THE INFLUENCE OF THE ROSE
ON GARDEN DESIGN

While roses had been grown in European gardens from mediaeval days onwards, they had been used as surrounding hedges or were cultivated for their medicinal and officinal values. We do not hear of their being used to create a rose garden until the forming of La Malmaison. Thus the Empress made gardening history in no small way.

The design of Joséphine's garden was something of a novelty in garden layout. It embodied nothing of the mediaeval knot, nor of the French *parterre de broderie,* nor was it related in any way to the *Jardin Anglais* which had recently become popular across northern Europe from its English inception. Her garden was designed so that the individual beauties of plants could best be appreciated; in 1838, in his *The Suburban Gardener and Villa Companion,* J. C. Loudon described this new idea as Gardenesque – as a counterpart to the Picturesque of the late eighteenth century. I have read that he travelled in Europe after the Napoleonic wars and it is tempting to think that he may have visited Malmaison.

That Joséphine gathered together about 258 kinds of rose is proof of the fact that her aim was to have a garden of roses. After all, no other genus of hardy plants or shrubs was at that time available with so great a number of species and selected garden varieties. Her garden may therefore be considered to rank as the first devoted to one genus, in a style which is the basis of much of our garden design today. And I think we may add that our present enthusiasm – craze, if you wish – was started by her and has ever since continued with increasing momentum.

It will be as well to look briefly at the state of gardening in Britain. At the time when Joséphine was creating her garden at La Malmaison, shrubs and flowers had been relegated to the walled kitchen gardens for about a hundred years, and so it continued through much of the nineteenth century. First the landscape reigned supreme and then, when Victorians wanted some colour and interest around the house, the lawns were given patterned beds, harking back to the days of the seventeenth-century parterres: they were filled with the new exotic "bedding plants" which could be nurtured in the new greenhouses, heated with coal, with plenty of garden labour to tend it all. Though flowering shrubs had been planted in some of the landscapes in the eighteenth century, they did not assume much importance in the villa garden, their place being taken by the then comparatively new laurels, aucubas and rhododendrons. These were admirable for framing garden views.

As rose plants lessened in size through continuous breeding with the Chinese rose, it appeared that they were admirably fitted themselves to fill permanently the patterned beds on the lawn. This trend was accentuated by the rising cost of labour and the heating of greenhouses for bedding plants. William Paul considered that they would surpass in their flowering season an assembly of any other plants, even rhododendrons. (As he also grew rhododendrons this statement has some value.) Shirley Hibberd in his *The Amateur Rose Book* of 1874 claimed that "a rosarium worthy of its name is a good feature in a garden . . . and will prove to be the most popular of all features, not excepting even the American Garden" (rhododendrons and allied plants).

It is in Hibberd's book that we read about sunken rose gardens. This is once again the substituting of roses for dwarf plants in a parterre, which should always be looked down upon, from the windows of a house or a raised walk or mount, both of which had been popular in the seventeenth century.

The evergreen shrubberies created seclusion for the rose garden, because it must be admitted that few of the roses bred before 1890 or thereabouts were suitably compact for bedding. The Bourbons and Hybrid Perpetuals were mostly very tall, the Chinas weak, and the early Hybrid Teas a mixed bag; they all gave at least two crops of bloom, however, whereas nearly all of the old European hybrids flowered at midsummer only and were big and bulky as well. For seven or eight months of the year the rose garden, unless bolstered by small spring bulbs, must have given little delight.

Period rose gardens

Three rose gardens dating from around the turn of the century can still be visited today. In spite of their prowess in raising new roses during the nineteenth century, the French have always been more interested in garden design than in the plants themselves; we can go to the country around Paris to see two period-piece gardens. The Roseraie de l'Haÿ was laid out by Edouard André, editor of the *Revue Horticole*, for Jules Gravereaux, the originator of the Bon Marché shops. Apart from a little up-dating, this garden remains substantially as it was, a mirror of garden design and the choice of roses of the period. The other garden, Bagatelle, was designed by J. C. N. Forestier in 1907. The former is a roughly triangular plot containing arched vistas and a dense array of beds, all filled solely with roses. The latter is a gracious formal design, punctuated with topiary, within a beautiful park. About 1900 the German National rosarium was laid out at Sangerhausen, now in East Germany. This is less formal but contains a prodigious number of varieties.

The two French gardens are impeccably maintained by the State and both exhibit every known way of displaying roses. Many of the beds are surrounded by box edging and may even have clipped grass in them around the roses. There are arches, treillage, pillars, swags, rustic work, standards and weeping standards. This is something that has only been done with the one genus, *Rosa*, and has been copied in Britain. It is as if we cannot have enough roses. Until the hybridizing began with ramblers of the Synstylae section, and climbing "sports" of other roses cropped up, there were very few rambling and climbing roses. Even so they could not be given the walls in the kitchen garden which were fully covered with fruit trees, so these artificial means of displaying them upon supports gathered favour. This is another example of how the Rose had influence upon garden design.

Many of the more perpetual-flowering of the new hybrid roses were weak growers, and were even recommended to be planted at 22–25 cm (9–10 inches) apart. Greater height was needed for some of the beds. Just as the bedding plant schemes had needed taller "dot" plants, so was the rose made to follow suit by being budded on stems of an understock – usually stout shoots of Dog rose dug out of the hedgerows. Thus quarter-, half-, and full-standards were born; when interspersed among the dwarf roses a four-tier system evolved, creating something quite new, a bank of colour. The rambler roses were given extra tall stems – in the French gardens they are neatly pruned into mops – and in England the metal umbrella was a new scheme which gave rise to "weeping" standards. With no other genus has such artificiality reigned.

This use of the roses for garden display was not what was admired by Dean Hole and the Reverend Honeywood d'Ombrain, and others of the founders of the (Royal) National Rose Society. Their ideal was a series of long straight beds containing rows of different kinds of mainly Hybrid Perpetual roses, with one desire: the production of prize blooms for the show bench.

Neither style pleased William Robinson. Against these ideals he launched his fulminations in *The English Flower Garden* in 1883, and elsewhere in his prolific writings. There is no doubt that, starting life as he did in the potting shed, so to speak, he educated himself to a high degree and was able during his long life to write very convincingly about many and varied aspects of gardening. He abhorred roses in beds by themselves and advocated growing them in mixture with other plants. He claimed that the rightful beauty of many of the old garden roses was, by excess pruning, being denied them; in fact, that many of them were being given up in preference to little bushes which produced blooms for exhibition. Further he foretold early mortality in the new rose gardens because other plants should be grown around them in order to shade the soil. (Considering that one of the uses of hooked prickles is to hoist rose species above their neighbours, perhaps this is a pointer to the fact that roses thrive best where their soil is not baked by sunshine.)

His writings came in time to prepare the way for the pen of Gertrude Jekyll. From her *Roses for English Gardens* of 1902 is extracted the following quotation: "We are growing impatient of the usual rose garden, generally a sort of target of concentric rings of beds placed upon turf, often with no special aim at connected design with the portions of the garden immediately about it, and filled with plants without a thought of their colour effect or any other worthy attention". In her garden was developed another idea for the use of rambler roses: that of training them into trees, in order to achieve a natural effect instead of one that was artificial. Even so she was a great advocate of the sunken garden (not necessarily filled with roses), very often with a pergola surrounding it. But in the main she used the older Shrub roses, the stronger "bedding" roses and the newly introduced species to good effect as general garden furnishings.

Roses as flowering shrubs

It will be seen from the above that Miss Willmott's great rose book came just at the right time to call attention to the shrubby roses. We were at the parting of the ways. On the one hand were the nurserymen and many garden owners who found all they wanted in the then newly raised bush Hybrid Teas, and on the other hand there were a few enlightened and knowledgeable gardeners who realized what had gone before, and were anxious to continue with the cultivation of these plants. It was indeed the wild species that had been reaching our shores for several decades that helped the Rose to stage its latest significant influence on garden design, as a *flowering shrub*.

It so happened that around 1900 two splendid species were introduced from the wilds of China, *R. hugonis* and *R. moyesii*, clear canary-yellow and brilliant tomato- or blood-red respectively. Since the bulk of wild roses are of some shade of pink these struck a new note; they caused gardeners to realize that among roses were to be found species every bit as valuable as all the other ornamental shrubs which were arriving from around the Northern and Southern Hemispheres. It was these shrubs, noted for their flower, berry and autumn colour, which in the early twentieth century created something of a landslide towards informal gardening. The Rose may be said to have revealed itself as an important shrub between the wars, and still more by 1950, even though one of its most valuable species, *R. rugosa*, had been introduced 150 years before.

Yet another use for the rose is for ground-cover. There is a large bed at The Gardens of the Rose of the Royal National Rose Society at St Albans devoted to the prostrate and hummock-forming hybrids, which with their dense prickly growth provide a suitable deterrent to trespassers, both weeds and animals.

We have indeed come full circle. On the one hand is the fact that the design of The Gardens of the Rose, St Albans, by Harry Clacy, reveals very significantly the type of design favoured by the Empress Joséphine and J. C. Loudon: the Gardenesque. On the other hand, gardeners today often favour the traditional mixed array of mediaeval and Elizabethan days. It is a style which has lived, buffeted by fashion but undimmed, in the walled kitchen gardens of great houses and in the humblest of cottage gardens, where plants have always been appreciated for what they are and not necessarily for the effect they create.

ELLEN ANN WILLMOTT

The names "Willmott" and "Warley" have been indelibly written in my memory since as a schoolboy I purchased at 6d each plants of *Aethionema* 'Warley Hybrid' and *Campanula pusilla (cochleariifolia)* 'Miss Willmott' for my rock garden. And later I found *Ceratostigma willmottiana*, *Phlox decussata* 'Ellen Willmott' and *Rosa willmottiae* growing in the Cambridge Botanic Garden. I remember sowing seeds from her at the Botanic Garden in the late 1920s, and seeing and writing labels with the accession number and date on them at the top, with the magic name Willmott underneath.

I have long possessed *The Genus Rosa*, which I purchased in 1939 when it was remaindered at £6; *Warley Garden in Spring and Summer* was obtained considerably later. I was therefore more than a little honoured when I was asked to prepare this new edition of Alfred Parsons' paintings of her roses. The more so because, like Miss Willmott's, my life has been

so taken up with the beauty of plants (and especially roses), and with music and painting.

Many of the plants for which Miss Willmott received Awards of Merit from the Royal Horticultural Society are still well known in cultivation. Even as late as 1931 and 1933 the buttonholes she wore at the Shows of the Royal Horticultural Society were commented on. Sir William Lawrence, Bart., the then President of the Society, would note that "Miss Willmott wore…", in his occasional notes on the Shows in *Gardening Illustrated*.

It was not my good fortune ever to meet her, but I remember her spare figure, under average height, dressed mainly in black and with a sort of toque on her head. My task in writing these notes has been greatly lessened by having at my elbow a copy of Dr Audrey le Lièvre's *Miss Willmott of Warley Place*, published by Faber & Faber in 1980. This book is all that a biography should be, apart from its paucity of illustrations. It informs us about her entire life accurately and entertainingly; in fact I found it almost impossible to put down. Dr le Lièvre has succeeded in bringing almost to life again a person whose tumultuous energy and dynamic egoism, coupled with vast knowledge and great generosity, could hardly be imagined without such an aid. From it I have extracted dates and facts which have enabled me to write the following notes. To invoke her life and times you need Dr le Lièvre's book to visualize one who was at the summit of gardening alongside Gertrude Jekyll and William Robinson.

I will briefly sketch in her early life. Her father, Frederick Willmott, came of a family of chemists, but decided to devote his life to law and became a solicitor in Southwark. He married Ellen Fell, who was of the Tasker family. Ellen Ann was born in 1858, and Rose in 1861; there was also another daughter, Ada but, sadly, she died when young. In 1875 the family moved to Essex, purchasing Warley Place, not far from Brentwood. It had two lodges and about 30 acres of land, complete with meadows, stream and ancient ponds; later Mr Willmott purchased an adjoining farm, the total holding eventually covering some 60 acres. Frederick Willmott was deeply interested in the farm and the produce from it, and admired his garden and grounds.

The Willmotts brought up their daughters to live like ladies and to study the polite arts. Ellen excelled in all, with sister Rose a close second. By the time she was grown up, she could speak French, German and Italian, was an expert musician, playing the violin, viola, cello, organ and piano; she sang well, both in choral societies and the Bach Choir and was devoted to madrigal singing. She had beauty, intelligence, talent in many ways and the aptitude for complete absorption in whatever she was doing. Being blessed with a "fairy" godmother, Countess Tasker, from the age of seven onwards she found on her birthday breakfast plate a cheque for £1,000, the equivalent of about £24,700 today. This enabled her to indulge her fancies

Above: Ellen Ann Willmott, botanist and gardener; portrait by Rosina Mantovani.
Left: a view in the garden at Warley Place; and **below:** Warley Place, Great Warley, Essex – Miss Willmott's home for 59 years. Paintings by Alfred Parsons.

in painting in oils; she had tools for farrier's work and carpentry, a lathe and a printing press; a dark room for developing photographic plates and films, even in colour; a microscope and telescope.

Miss Willmott inherited some of her parents' love for gardens and flowers. In 1882 she set about making a large alpine garden, employing the noted York firm of James Backhouse & Son to start the construction, which they did in the then still popular millstone grit. Henri Correvon of Geneva became her friend and mentor; he was already famous for his work in acclimatizing plants of the Alps. The making of the rock garden involved much moving of soil and was so designed by Miss Willmott that, with the stream flowing through it, there were aspects and soils to suit any and every plant she wished to grow.

Mr Willmott died in 1892 and Mrs Willmott in 1898. But in 1888, at the age of thirty, Miss Willmott inerited £140,000, approximately £4½ million today, from Countess Tasker. She proceeded to collect plants of all kinds, as well as furniture and pictures, glass, china and silver; in fact, everything that appealed to her love of beauty.

Her sister, Rose, married into one of the oldest and wealthiest families in the country – the Berkeleys at Spetchley Park, Worcester, and Berkeley Castle in Gloucestershire. I recall being told that at one time in its history the family could hunt on its own land almost all the way from Berkeley to London! Rose died rather young, but I remember staying for the weekend at Spetchley some years after her death and on going round the splendid garden – and that at Berkeley – I realised that Rose had had the "touch" as well as Ellen.

It was not until 1894, when she was thirty-five, that Miss Willmott became a Fellow of the Royal Horticultural Society. A few years later she was elected to sit on the Narcissus and Tulip committee. This was a great honour and came about because she had already raised many hybrids of daffodils and was intensely interested also in tulips. It had been her good fortune to meet and exchange experiences with the Reverend C. Wolley-Dod (the portrait of whose rose is reproduced in this book), and the Reverend G. H. Engleheart, both daffodil specialists. It was at a time when the white daffodils were beginning to be selected; her efforts carried her forward for several years and by 1909, when she ceased hybridizing, her seedlings had found a ready market. It looks as if by this year roses had captivated her completely and apart from her every endeavour to make her garden more beautiful, particularly with shrubs and naturalized bulbs, she became deeply involved in the botany of roses. In the annals of horticulture it is rare to find one who derived as much interest and delight from botany as from her artistic placing of plants in her garden.

By this time the house at Warley was well staffed, from butler and housekeeper to three footmen downwards; there were several carriages and 104 gardeners, and apart from her head gardener and foremen, they received 18s per week. With the house running smoothly she was able to devote herself to the garden, and also to her other multifarious activities. Partly through her enterprise in sending out every year a list of seeds collected in her three gardens (she now also had the gardens at Menton and Ventimiglia), she was in touch with all the botanic gardens in the British Isles, and many abroad, and with innumerable leading figures in the gardening world. It is said that she grew 100,000 species and varieties of trees, shrubs and plants.

In the early years of this century Miss Willmott became very influential in gardening circles, presenting 15,000 sheets of herbarium specimens of European plants to Kew. With Sir Thomas Hanbury, in 1903, she became one of three Trustees for the Royal Horticultural Society's new garden at Wisley and two years later was elected to the Linnaean Society of London. Shares were taken in E. H. Wilson's expedition to Western China; William Robinson dedicated the 1907 volume of his periodical *The Garden* to her, and in the same year *The Botanical Magazine* did the same; this was a signal honour, and relates very forcefully to the fact that Ellen was a *botanical* as well as an artistic gardener. In fact it was the learned botanical people who chiefly fascinated her; she was scarcely interested in the owners of small gardens. A vast correspondence – in long hand – was kept going at the rate of more than a dozen letters a day. The mind boggles at how she could keep her musical activities and rehearsals, attend concerts and flower shows and still keep in exact touch with all that went on at Warley. She supported by her interest and subscriptions a long list of charities, horticultural and otherwise. Numbered among her friends and visitors were the highest in the land, including Queen Alexandra and later Queen Mary and the Princess Royal.

When the Royal Horticultural Society instituted the Victoria Medal of Honour in commemoration of Queen Victoria's Jubilee, they honoured Miss Willmott and Miss Jekyll, who were the only two women among the sixty recipients. With William Robinson they dominated British horticulture in many ways. All three were aiming at natural beauty in gardens. Gertrude Jekyll and Ellen Willmott had much in common, but while the former devoted herself to working for others through her books and garden designing, the latter tended to devote all to herself, continually advancing her ambitions and savouring the excitement of gardening with many botanical and horticultural leaders of the day. They both studied deeply the craft of gardening as well as the art. According to Miss Jekyll, Miss Willmott was "the greatest of all living women gardeners".

Miss Willmott's upbringing had included nothing to educate her to look after her income. With so vast an inheritance she spent and went on spending. She could not stop. Her own collection of roses enthralled her, she added continually to them with new species raised from seed collected from all parts of the world. I think she became obsessed with roses and determined to emulate the Empress Joséphine in producing a *magnum opus* devoted to the genus and to dedicate it to Queen Alexandra. The project was beyond her capabilities botanically and financially. To help with the botany she enlisted J. G. Baker of Kew. Nobody helped her financially. The work was illustrated by no less than Alfred Parsons, RA and contained 154 paintings. The book shows the very real awakening of a great gardener to the manifold beauties of the rose and is a landmark in horticultural history. It falls just short of the word "great" in view of its mistakes, inconsistencies and limitations, but we must remember that its promoter, keen botanist that she was, had not had the benefit of a scientific education.

The Genus Rosa came out between 1910 and 1914, in parts at £1 each. The colour printing was not good; yellow pervaded to excess all tints of flower and leaf. The sales promotion seems, according to today's methods, to have been rather lacking and the onset of the Great War reduced its success. Little profit was made by author or publishers; probably the collaborators came off as well as anyone. Miss Willmott had reached the summit of her career. Like so many great operas her life started in sunshine and glitter and was to end in gloom and humiliation – but never in despair. She had too stout a heart, too much enthusiasm for her beloved plants and music for that. Her staff gradually left and she was unable to afford to recruit more. But honours were still to come to her, coupled with sadness and bereavement.

Had she devoted her energies solely to Warley Place garden all might have been well, but in addition to this large holding she had indulged her desires for a château and garden, Tresserve, and later yet another, Boccanegra. These two gardens on that sun-drenched coast enabled her to grow out of doors innumerable exotics which could only thrive under glass in Essex. She spent untold sums of money on both gardens as well as the houses, filled with rare and costly furniture and all that went with it, and had the terrible double expense of re-stocking Tresserve when it caught fire; it had not been insured.

Eventually the two properties abroad were sold; mortgages were taken out on various parts of the Wa ley holdings; Sir Frank Crisp and other friends lent moneys and gave sureties, but it was all to little avail except that it kept away the bailiffs. Miss Willmott of Warley Place simply could not economize; whatever troubles beset her vanished as she tended her garden. She was honoured with the Dean Hole Medal, awarded by the (Royal) National Rose Society, and by the Royal Horticultural Society by being asked to sit on further committees. For thirty years her famous seed list had been sent out with sometimes more than six hundred names of plants on it. And yet many gardeners today know nothing about her career, nor the international flame that burned so brightly during the late 19th century and the first quarter of this century, to gutter out like a burnt-down candle at last, though with spirit as high as ever.

Year by year distinguished old friends died but she kept going until the last. In the spring of 1934 she was singing in Bach's St Matthew Passion; in September, suddenly, and without the discomfort of losing her mobility and ability, she died at the age of 76.

But you must read Dr le Lièvre's book to realize to the full how she had lived, enjoying and collecting everything rare, beautiful and expensive. Though she disposed of a few treasures to help her in her last years, her motto had been, I think, "To have and to hold". There is no doubt that life had given her great satisfaction even though the understanding of good husbandry and economy eluded her. And those of us who have come after her cannot but bless her for commissioning Alfred Parsons to depict her roses in these portraits, so true to life.

Thinking to add a little first-hand experience to these notes I visited the site of her garden in March 1986. The property is at present in the care of the Essex Naturalist Trust, and is owned by Mr Norman Carter. The meadows outside her garden were purple from millions of wild-type *Crocus vernus*; elsewhere were thousands of snowdrops, mostly *Galanthus nivalis*, intermarried here and there with *G. byzantinus*; in the walled garden they vied in beauty with sheets of rich blue *Scilla bifolia* and patches of aconites. The proud house had been pulled down but the basements and some tessellated flooring remain. The mighty millstone grit boulders from Yorkshire still give shape to the splendid gorge of the alpine garden. But nearly everywhere is covered by fifty-year-old sycamore seedlings, vast carpets of *Hedera colchica* and a few coarse bamboos.

A Fancy from Fontenelle
"De mémoires de roses on n'a point vu mourir le Jardinier."

*The Rose in the garden slipped her bud,
And she laughed in the pride of her youthful blood,
As she thought of the Gardener standing by –
"He is old, – so old! And he soon must die!"*

*The full Rose waxed in the warm June air,
And she spread and spread till her heart lay bare;
And she laughed once more as she heard his tread –
"He is older now! He will soon be dead!"*

*But the breeze of the morning blew, and found
That the leaves of the blown Rose strewed the ground;
And he came at noon, that Gardener old,
And he raked them gently under the mould.*

*And I wove the thing to a random rhyme,
For the Rose is Beauty, the Gardener, Time.*

Austin Dobson, London, 1885.

ALFRED PARSONS AND *THE GENUS ROSA*

BRYAN N BROOKE MD, M Chir, FRCS, Hon FRACS
President, Medical Art Society, 1979-83

Although in 1921 Miss Ellen Willmott expressed her fear that she might suffer the "discredit" of having her book remaindered, the tide has since turned with a vengeance. Graham Stuart Thomas bought the two volumes of *The Genus Rosa* for £6 in 1939: it is now a collector's piece fetching close on £800, when it appears on the market. The quarto volumes are imposing in size and binding and *The Genus Rosa* exudes the feeling of a generous work, of no expense having been spared – nor was it. But the book is flawed, as I discovered when I was at last able to obtain the work (for £48) in about 1950.

Alfred Parsons was my great uncle, and I knew his work well for his paintings were admired and had been collected by my family. He was a fine colourist in both oil and watercolour, and an accurate, sensitive draughtsman, although these gifts were not immediately apparent in the printed volumes of *The Genus Rosa* which, to say the least, were disappointing.

It was from Wilfred Blunt's *Art of Botanical Illustration* that I discovered that all his original paintings had been acquired for the Royal Horticultural Society by the Cory Bequest. There, in the Lindley Library, they are to be found each pasted opposite its respective reproduction; the contrast between the reproductions and the originals is as astonishing as it is reassuring. Blunt's observations that Parsons had been ill-served by the lithographer are fully vindicated. The subtlety of the original colours has been lost in the chromolithography, and the delicacy of the drawing in the crudity of the reproduction.

Alfred Parsons produced 132 paintings yet the standard never faltered; as a whole they present a masterpiece comparable with the work of Redouté. It became my intent that Parsons' greatest work should be brought to light by modern reproduction; the realization has taken 30 years. One question remains: why did Parsons, an experienced and knowledgeable illustrator, not supervise the lithography more carefully? The answer lies in the history of the genesis of *The Genus Rosa* and of Parsons himself.

Alfred Parsons was born in 1847 in Somerset where his father, a doctor, practised in Beckington. Dr Joshua Parsons was a noted expert on perennial and rock plants, and was a friend of William Robinson, founder and publisher of *The Garden* magazine. The doctor liked to paint his flowers; the few examples of his work which remain today are exquisitely and tenderly drawn, and most carefully painted. There is no doubt

where Alfred acquired both his ability, his interest and his inclination – and at least one important connection, for he became a horticulturist and a close friend of Robinson also.

Alfred was one of a large family and his father was not well off so, at the age of sixteen, after a rather informal education even for those times, he found himself sitting at a desk in the Post Office Savings Bank. Four years he endured, then broke away for a more welcome stool and easel, spurred on to a greater application to drawing and its disciplines which now came as a particular pleasure to him. Twenty years later he had established himself as an illustrator for *Harper's Magazine*, and as a landscape gardener. He advised on laying out the garden at Wightwick Manor, designed by William Morris and now owned by the National Trust.

Dr Parsons was noted for his gentleness, unselfishness and lovable disposition. Alfred appears to have taken after his father, and was generous into the bargain. Certainly his association with the "Broadway Group" seems to confirm this.

The Broadway Group is a *post hoc* concept; the members certainly did not see themselves as a special association of artists. The Group came about in 1885 when Laurence Hutton, the literary editor of *Harper's*, wished to place his chief illustrators, Francis David Millet and Edwin Austin Abbey, close to Stratford-upon-Avon at a time of romanticism with a high regard for Shakespearian inspiration. Alfred shared his house in London at Bedford Gardens with Millet and his family (Parsons was a bachelor and remained so throughout his life). He accompanied the Millets to Broadway, where he met Henry Harper and so began his contact with the magazine. He got to know Abbey as a close friend, and lent his London studio to him and to John Singer Sargent.

On this evidence it would be difficult to deny that Parsons was a generous and sociable man. The Group soon attracted literary figures like Henry James, Comyns Carr and Edmund Gosse, and painters such as Lawrence Alma-Tadema and John Singer Sargent. They gathered year after year, and Alfred played his part as host at picnics up the Thames in his steam launch and even at his home in Frome. The idyll could not last. The intrusion of Gertrude Mead, who married Ned Abbey in 1891, broke the spell, and after the marriage the couple moved away to Fairford, in Gloucestershire.

It must have been shortly after this that Parsons

began to paint the roses in Ellen Willmott's gardens at Great Warley, and in France and Italy, for by 1901 she already had 40 paintings in hand. This is evident from a letter from the publisher John Murray, dated 16 May 1901,

> "I understand that Mr Parsons is employed by you to paint the roses as they blossom and reach perfection: that he has actually done some 40 of the 140 but that he can of course only work at stated seasons, and that, as the roses do not necessarily bloom according to scientific classes, there will be difficulties in the way of producing the parts in any scientific sequence, and at fixed dates." (John Murray archives, London.)

This letter constituted the only business arrangement between Murray's and Miss Ellen Willmott for the next nine years. Miss Willmott was commissioning the work and paying for it to be published. All Murray could expect was five per cent of the profit on each full set of 24 parts sold to monthly subscribers, after which the complete work would be sold in two volumes.

One difficulty was soon on its way: Parsons preferred one printer for his illustrations, Murray another. Parsons was not best pleased to discover that Murray was answerable directly to Miss Willmott just as he was, so that the choice of printer was not his. Parsons backed the claims of Whitehead, who presented an estimate twice as expensive as Murray's candidate, Grigg. He continued to press those claims, misguidedly since it was known that he had a commercial interest in the firm who would supply the paper to Whitehead. He was no more successful in persuading Miss Willmott to his way than he was in bending Murray to it. He then began a campaign to denigrate the work of Grigg; he poured scorn upon proofs arranged by Murray, and wrote to Miss Willmott alleging, inaccurately, that they were printed on inferior paper. He sent a sample for analysis and would not release the report. Murray's reaction was to note: "Parsons's letter is, I think, libellous and if it were not for Miss Willmott's sake he deserves to be punished for it."

Of Parsons' venality there can be no doubt. What can have taken possession of him? He was not a malevolent man, yet his behaviour was inexcusable. And when he died he was said to have been one of the most popular of the Royal Academicians. *The Times* obituary contained a clue. In 1914 Parsons was elected President of the Royal Society of Water Colour Painters, remaining in office until his death, and *The Times* referred to his business capacity which made him invaluable to his colleagues. Parsons' background had provided no guarantee of comfort, and through necessity he had become successful in business. His decision to leave the bank for the uncertainty of a career as a painter must have reinforced earlier feelings of insecurity. Although it was not long before his illustrations and his landscape gardening began to meet his needs, and more, the need to grasp any and

every opportunity had become ingrained. It would be less than surprising if Parsons saw a double chance of financial reward in his association with *The Genus Rosa*. Moreover it would be understandable that the painter should feel that he had the right to choose the materials for the printing of his work and that he should prefer a supplier he already used and trusted.

For well over a year he had insisted on his own choice and failed to give due consideration to John Murray's wiser counsels. On receiving the report which completely vindicated the printer, Grigg, he could not bring himself to admit to being in the wrong; he placed the Atlantic between himself and those he had so wantonly accused. From then on Parsons had neither the influence nor the inclination to maintain close supervision of the chromolithography. Shortly after Christmas 1902 a grudging apology, sufficient to avoid a possible libel suit, reached Murray from Parsons in New York.

He never again expressed dissatisfaction with the paper or the printer: he could not afford to do otherwise. He appears to have taken up an attitude of acquiesence, permitting himself an occasional "I told you so", as in 1907 when some loss of colour was noted by Miss Willmott in one or two of the plates. Parsons kept a low profile while he and Murray kept their distance. Rapprochement had to await the completion of the work in March 1914 when Parsons had the grace to write and congratulate him. Murray thanked him warmly for writing, after "so many difficulties and vexatious delays it is very pleasant to receive your words of commendation".

The vexatious delays were all of Miss Willmott's doing. She was not an easy person and was used to having her own way with a tendency to blame faults of her own making onto others; not for nothing has the prickly *Eryngium giganteum* received the alternative appellation "Miss Willmott's Ghost". She was dilatory, disorganized and indecisive at crucial moments and she was too often abroad when action was most needed, with the result that the gestation of *The Genus Rosa* lasted until 1914. It could have been published within five years of the 1901 "contract" letter, for the intended 120 paintings were completed long before then.

By 1908, after years of requests, Murray still had not received Miss Willmott's letterpress to accompany the illustrations, nor was he receiving payment for his outgoings. By 1908 she was borrowing £500 from him after a fire at her property in France which she had failed to insure; by 1919 she was begging for loans to cover personal expenses that had nothing to do with the book, the security in her mind being the 740 unsold copies of *The Genus Rosa*, for none of which had she paid Murray. Neither would she make up her mind as to the publication date of the first set in 1910, holding back copies from review, hoping to manipulate editors into using reviewers of her choice, since, "it will be given to someone who knows nothing of the subject (hardly anyone does know Roses) and the review will simply be for Parsons' drawing and other minor features of the book which will be a great pity".

In May 1903 Ellen Willmott had ordered 1,000 copies to be printed of the book, which when completed in 1914 comprised 25 parts, 132 coloured illustrations and, apart from the glossary, 19 drawings of heps by Phyllis Parsons, Alfred's niece, and 64 by Miss Williamson, an art mistress at a girls' school. By the time the first part appeared in 1910 the estimated cost of the 1,000 sets was £5,275; the final cost must have been considerably more. To this Miss Willmott contributed over £1,500, the brunt being borne by the long-suffering John Murray. In return, he can have received little more than £900 from the 260 sets that were sold. In today's terms publication cost over £500,000, and the original price of the complete work in two volumes was £26 7s 0d – over £750 today.

There is a sad footnote to the history of *The Genus Rosa*. Throughout the Great War attempts were made to fulfil Miss Willmott's ambition that her work should receive recognition in America, by finding a publisher willing to buy copies; against the odds Murray obtained offers which still gave her a profit. The offers were turned down, and when Alfred Parsons died in January 1920, at the age of 72, there were still 740 copies in the publisher's hands.

Murray preserved and received a further offer for all the remaining sets from Duttons of New York at a price that would have more than reimbursed Miss Willmott though not him, but she procrastinated. A year passed and Duttons wrote to Murray that markets had become unfavourable so they must cancel the order. Miss Willmott at last made up her mind in favour, but too late by one month to the day.

Age and financial worries were beginning to tell on Ellen Willmott; she started to bite the hand that had been so helpful to her, with wild and extravagant accusations; of demanding an exorbitant commission; of doing nothing to sell the book: of anything she could turn her mind to – and all untrue. In February 1922 came a last gasp of exasperation from the generous and patient John Murray: "if other books were to involve half the trouble that this one has, we might as well put up our shutters . . . we have not only done everything that a publisher could do to help you, but we have far exceeded what are the normal duties of a publisher".

This book presents Alfred Parsons in a new light. Modern reproduction has at last done justice to his originals and my hope is now achieved: that one day a wider public – even on this occasion in America – might have the opportunity to enjoy his masterpiece.

Alfred Parsons photographed in his studio, c.1885

Rose 'Aimée Vibert'

Rosa × alba 'Céleste'

Rosa × alba 'Semiplena'

Rose 'Andersonii'

Rose 'Anemone'

Rosa anemoniflora

Rosa arvensis

Rosa banksiae 'Lutea'

Rose 'Blanche Moreau'

Rosa blanda

Rosa bracteata

Rosa brunonii

Rosa californica 'Plena'

Rose 'Calocarpa'

Rosa carolina

Rosa centifolia 'Bullata'

Rosa centifolia 'Cristata'

Rosa centifolia 'Muscosa'

Rosa centifolia pomponia

Rosa centifolia 'Variegata'

Rosa chinensis 'Miss Willmott's Crimson China'

Rosa chinensis 'Mutabilis'

Rosa damascena 'Hebe's Lip'

Rose 'Dupontii'

Rosa ecae

Rosa fedtschenkoana

Rose 'Fellenberg'

Rosa foetida

Rosa foetida 'Bicolor'

Rosa × fortuneana

Rose 'Fortune's Double Yellow'

Rosa gallica

Rosa gallica 'Versicolor'

Rosa gallica 'Violacea'

Rosa gigantea

Rosa glauca

Rosa × hardii

Rosa hemisphaerica

Rosa × hibernica

Rosa hugonis

Rosa × jacksonii

Rose 'Janet's Pride'

Rosa laevigata

Rosa × lheritierana

Rose 'Macrantha'

Rosa macrophylla

Rosa macrophylla × R. rugosa

Rosa majalis

Rosa moyesii

Rosa multiflora

Rosa nitida

Rose 'Old Blush China'

Rosa pendulina

Rosa persica

Rosa pimpinellifolia 'Andrewsii'

Rosa pimpinellifolia 'Grandiflora'

Rosa pimpinellifolia var. *myriacantha*

Rosa roxburghii 'Roxburghii'

Rosa sempervirens

Rosa sericea

Rosa setigera

Rosa soulieana

Rose 'Stanwell Perpetual'

Rosa stellata

Rosa virginiana

Rosa virginiana 'Alba'

Rosa webbiana

Rosa wichuraiana

Rosa willmottiae

Rose 'Wolley-Dod'

In the notes accompanying the plates, a percentage is given at the foot of each page.
This denotes the size of the plate in proportion to the original painting.

Having been raised in 1828 in France, and being a rambler rose almost without scent, it might be thought this rose would have gone out of cultivation. But it has been saved by various facts. From *Rosa sempervirens* it inherits the most glossy, dark green and beautiful of all rose foliage. From *R. moschata*, the Musk rose, it inherits its late and repeat-flowering habit. And because of a Noisette rose ('Champney's Pink Cluster') in its parentage, it was classed as a Noisette and thus was included in this highly desired class in the mid-nineteenth century. Had it inherited the glorious fragrance of the Musk rose, it would have been even more treasured. Its vigour, luxuriant foliage and prolific late-summer and autumn flowering place it in a class all of its own, and it is consequently a unique rose that seems to offer much to the hybridists without their being aware of it. The commercial aspect, of course, enters into the matter; hundreds more bush roses are sold than ramblers and hence there is less profit in them for the raiser. The fact that prickles are very sparingly produced is another fact in its favour and if only we could find again 'Aimée Vibert à fleur jaune' it would be welcomed with open arms. This variant was probably a "sport", introduced in 1904; the salmon-orange flowers were depicted in the *Journal des Roses* in May 1905.

There is a remarkable photograph of the original in Gertrude Jekyll's *Roses for English Gardens* of 1902, showing it "balloon-trained" on iron arches, a veritable mound of blossom, attesting to the suitability of its synonym 'Bouquet de la Mariée'. I prefer to grow it on a sunny wall, however, because its shoots are sometimes spoiled by a cold winter, and the warmth from the wall helps the later crops of flowers. It grows and flowers well at Mottisfont.

Rose Aimée Vibert

This peerless rose has endeared itself to everyone by its pure soft pink flowers, which tone so well with the greyish leaves. Parsons has captured well the shapely bud which has no equal among roses unless we contemplate 'Cécile Brunner' and the 'Rose d'Amour'. It is most fortunate that the bush is so strong and healthy, being almost as vigorous as *Rosa* × *alba* 'Semiplena', with the same pale green twigs, large prickles and foliage of Dog rose quality, but larger. And the fragrance: all the most representative roses of the Alba group have a fresh sweet scent which to my nose is only equalled in its clarity by Lily of the Valley.

'Céleste' is attributed to the Dutch and was known at the end of the eighteenth century, so that it is strange it has apparently no known Dutch name, though the Latin *incarnata* crops up in the history of Alba roses fairly frequently. While to us today this rose is distinguished from other pink roses of the Alba group, this has not always been so; it has been confused with 'Maiden's Blush' in some old books. 'Maiden's Blush' was known prior to the fifteenth century and is another tough old rose of similar growth and qualities. Its flowers are fully double, opening from unpropitious buds of a creamy tint to a flat array of short petals, pink towards the centre but almost white around the circumference of the flower, and in my estimation it is surpassingly sweet-scented. But the queen of all is one which owes some of its beauty once again to a Damask rose: 'Koenigin von Danemarck' of 1826. In this is the richest colouring of the White roses, the most sumptuous doubling and quartering and an unforgettable scent.

Truly the White roses rank very high among the old roses, their qualities perfected by selection before the adulteration that came about through the China rose, whatever other advantages may have accrued from this species.

95%

Rosa x alba 'Céleste'

As with the oldest Gallica and Damask roses, the origin of the White rose is lost in what are generally called the "mists of time". The rose depicted by Parsons is undoubtedly what we grow today as *Rosa*× *alba* 'Semiplena', but just when this originated is not known. During its long life it has "sported" to the fully double white 'Maxima', which in turn has reverted to 'Semiplena' in plants under my care, and recently at Mottisfont it produced a branch with flowers of only five petals. Unfortunately this branch died before it had been propagated.

These roses are very different from the hybrid Gallicas and Damasks and their relatives, showing, in their smooth green wood and the few large, hooked prickles, an influence which is always attributed to *R. canina*, the Dog rose, as are its hard, greyish leaves. It is generally believed to be a hybrid of the Summer Damask with a white-flowered geographical form or botanical variety of *R. canina*. Such roses occur in eastern Europe and western Asia and are known as *R. corymbifera* or *R. dumetorum*.

It seems fairly certain that one of the White roses formed the badge of the House of York, while the Red Rose of Lancaster is considered to be *R. gallica officinalis*; since the latter spreads readily by suckers, a plant might well have invaded a bush of *R. alba* and enabled the disputing nobles to have picked flowers of either colour from apparently the one bush. We have no means of proving this; the York and Lancaster rose (*R. damascena versicolor*) bore pink, white and particoloured flowers all on the same bush. It was known prior to 1629, though the other two claimants to historic fame are much older and therefore more eligible.

R. × *alba* 'Semiplena' is a very vigorous, woody, stout shrub and will grow readily to 2.4m (8ft) or more, and as wide, and is extremely long-lived. In Bulgaria it is grown as a sort of hedge around the fields of Damask roses, but does not produce such pure attar.

93%

Rosa x alba 'Semiplena'

Those who enjoy the beauty of *Rosa canina*, the Dog brier of our hedgerows, can hardly fail to be impressed with this more fully coloured hybrid of it. I would not suggest that its richer colouring makes it *better* than the blush pink of the Dog rose; we are all too prone in these days to extol the brighter colours, forgetting sometimes that a delicate tint holds something in itself which is not attained when the colour is intensified. Be this as it may, 'Andersonii' creates a more distinctive display than *R. canina*, because its flowers are larger, of richer pink, are borne more freely and less widely spaced. In fact it can be one of the most spectacular of all. The leaves are of dark leaden green, hairy beneath (those of *R. canina* are smooth), and the heps are oval, brilliant scarlet and conspicuous.

As a shrub for a two-season display it can hold its own with most others; it is best for the wilder parts of the garden, making a large, prickly, arching bush about 1.8m (6ft) high by at least 2.4m (8ft) wide. It can also be trained into and over a hedge or small tree with great effect. It is nice to feel that one of our native roses has contributed so valuable a shrub to our gardens.

Nothing is known of its origin, except that it was first listed by Hillier & Sons of Winchester in 1912 and was thus very new when painted by Parsons. It is probably a hybrid with a garden rose.

Rose Andersonii

ROSE 'ANEMONE'

(*Rosa anemonoides* or 'Sinica Anemone')

This lovely rose is accredited to J. C. Schmidt of Erfurt in Germany, a rather surprising location, considering that its two parents are tender. Presumably they would have been grown under glass: they are reputed to have been *Rosa laevigata*, which is pretty certain, and a Tea rose. The date of raising is given as 1895 or 1896. Schmidt was the raiser also of 'Veilchenblau', the so-called "blue rambler"; its fragrance and its colour have endeared it to gardeners since 1909.

'Anemone' is a rose of great beauty and charm. It inherits some of the glossiness of its foliage from both parents, but it will be noticed that its leaflets are in threes, as in *R. laevigata*. The fragrant blooms are borne over a long period, but not abundantly, on a sparse-growing climbing plant which needs a warm sunny wall to give of its best, though it is hardy in itself. The soft clear pink of the flowers is enhanced by delicate veining.

In 1913 a "sport" occurred in California with flowers of a darker colour; I think a glowing cerise-crimson is fairly adequate for so startling a flower. Moreover, the reverse of the petals is much paler and in some lights appears to be grey. It is otherwise an exact counterpart of 'Anemone', and is called 'Ramona'.

These roses start flowering very early in the rose season, with for instance the Banksian roses, but continue intermittently for some weeks or even months. Being sparse of growth they are perhaps best when allowed to ramble through another sun-loving shrub on a warm wall.

88%

Rose Anemone

There is no other rose that bears a resemblance to this, found in a garden in Shanghai in 1844 by Robert Fortune. He was one of the first Britons to travel abroad in direct endeavour to discover new plants for a nursery firm – Standish & Noble of Bagshot, later Sunningdale Nurseries. (The two partners are remembered by *Lonicera standishii* and *Rhododendron × Nobleanum*, and we shall come across the firm again under Rose 'Fortune's Double Yellow'.)

This rose is possibly a hybrid between *Rosa banksiae* and *R. multiflora*; single-flowered plants have been found in Fokien Province of China, but there is no proof about its origin. The three leaflets, however, certainly point to *R. banksiae* being a parent.

In England this plant requires a warm climate and does best on a sunny wall, but is not much grown, in spite of the charm in shape and colour of the flowers, which, though double, have at first sight the appearance of apple blossom.

It would probably thrive best when growing through another shrub, a *Ceanothus* for instance, which would give it some protection, and also support for its long shoots.

Rosa anemoniflora

ROSA ARVENSIS

The English Musk Rose

This is a fairly common rose in southern England, and here and there in Ireland; otherwise it is found freely through Europe to central Turkey. Its sweet scent was mentioned more than once by Shakespeare and also by Spenser. It is usually found in bosky places and overgrown hedgerows, threading through the shrubs and into small trees, its long trails often purplish. Thence it hangs down and produces bunches of the single milk-white flowers just as the Dog rose (*Rosa canina*) is fading. The creamy yellow stamens bend inwards and turn blackish after pollination. The dark green leaves and rounded or oval red heps are characteristic of this species, which is seldom seen in gardens – presumably because of its short flowering season and unmanageable long trailing shoots.

On the other hand it has considerable potential to the hybridist for its ability to grow and flower well in shady places, even under trees. This it has transmitted to at least one well-known garden plant known as the Ayrshire 'Splendens'. This has great vigour and is extremely floriferous, with loosely double flowers, reddish in bud, opening to creamy pink. I have had it growing in my garden, hanging 3m (10ft) trails out of an old pear tree which in turn was in the shade of a huge oak. William Paul, the famous nurseryman and raiser of roses, wrote of this remarkable propensity as long ago as 1888, but it has never been taken to heart by hybridists. The origin of 'Splendens' is wrapped in mystery; it is possibly a hybrid of *R. arvensis* and *R. sempervirens* crossed with a golden rose of the nineteenth century. But neither species has the extraordinary fragrance of 'Splendens'; which has earned for it the name of Myrrh-scented rose. The other Ayrshire roses often possess no fragrance and their relationship with Ayrshire is rather tenuous. It is reported that the Earl of Loudon, who lived in Ayrshire, received in 1767 seeds from Canada, where both *R. arvensis* and *R. sempervirens* may have been taken by early settlers, and that these had become hybridized.

The true Musk rose of the ancients is *R. moschata*; although a species of the same section of roses (the Synstylae, with the styles united into a column instead of being free), it may be a native of southern Europe and North Africa. The flowers have an unforgettable sweet scent, reminiscent of musk – a rare and costly perfume obtained from the little Musk deer of northern India. It is a large sprawling shrub. Its flowers appear from midsummer onwards; thus this species also has value to hybridists and offers indeed one of the reasons why certain old European roses, such as the Autumn Damask, flower through summer and autumn.
R. moschata grows and flowers well at Mottisfont.

84%

Rosa arvensis

ROSA BANKSIAE 'LUTEA'

Banksian Rose

A spring-flowering rambling rose, which adds its soft yellow colouring to many a wall-grown Chinese *Wisteria* in Britain. The two make a delicate contrast and it is as a wall specimen in warmer districts that this rose is usually found. Though hardy, it needs all the sun's warmth to encourage it to flower well. This is rather odd, because its single white type apparently flowers as far north as Beijing (Peking). The double yellow form is most frequently seen in British gardens and is no doubt an old Chinese garden favourite; it arrived from China in 1824. Strangely, the single white form of the species, 'Normalis', had arrived earlier, in 1796, but was planted on the wall of Megginch Castle, Strathtay, Scotland, where it grew well but never flowered. Cuttings were taken to Nice where in the warm sunshine they flowered well. A double white form 'Alba Plena' was introduced from Canton in 1807 and a single yellow 'Lutescens' later in the nineteenth century. They all have flowers about 2.5cm (1in) across.

The two singles and also the double white have a penetrating and delicious perfume; the double yellow is also fragrant – a delicate primrose-like scent. Dean Hole, the famous rosarian-founder of the (Royal) National Rose Society, wrote of the double white that it had "a sweet perfume as though it had just returned from a visit to a Violet".

Willing as I should be to give wall space to any and all of them, I have to remember that they are very strong growers and cannot easily be curtailed. It is of course quite easy to cut their long green thornless shoots, but flowers are only produced on side shoots from two-year-old wood and thereafter. The answer is to remove a few big old branches every year and to tie-in the wayward thinner wood. They really only give of their best in exceptional circumstances. There was recorded in 1956 an immense specimen of the double yellow in Tombstone, Arizona, covering over 370 square metres (4,000 square feet), supported on posts and rails. I have yet to experience its flowering.

Rosa banksiae is possibly a parent of *R. anemoniflora*.

Rosa banksiae 'Lutea'

This was painted by Parsons and entitled *Rosa centifolia albo-muscosa*, but this name is incorrect. It is a hybrid between a mossy variety of the Autumn Damask rose and 'Comtesse de Murinais', which was a Damask Moss, and not a Centifolia Moss.

It is not generally appreciated that the pink Autumn Damask rose – which may well be of Roman origin, and is so called because it is distinct in flower-habit from the Summer Damask, of which 'York and Lancaster' is a variant – "sported" to a mossy variety with white flowers in 1835. It was known under the resounding title of 'Quatre Saisons Blanc Mousseux' or *R. damascena bifera alba muscosa*. In my care it has reverted on several occasions to the pink-flowered Autumn Damask, which probably owes its repeat-flowering habit to *R. moschata*, the Musk rose, which is presumed to be in its ancient parentage. The "moss" on the Damask rose is harsh, even prickly to the touch. Because it flowers intermittently until autumn and sets seeds (not being so fully double as the Centifolia moss), it gave rise to many hybrids.

'Blanche Moreau' was raised in 1880 and shows something of both moss variants – the less soft moss, the smaller foliage and flower and the occasional late bloom all point to the Autumn Damask moss. The confused story of the parentage and origin of all the ancient moss rose variants is given in detail by Dr C. C. Hurst in my book *The Old Shrub Roses*. Let me add here that in spite of the repeat-flowering habit, none of the hybrid moss roses measures up to the superlative quality and grace of the original Centifolia Moss rose and its "sport", 'Shailer's White'.

Rose 'Blanche Moreau'

The Hudson Bay or Labrador rose is obviously hardy, coming as it does from such northern latitudes (it also extends as far west as Vancouver), but it is seldom grown. It is not a distinguished-looking rose for our gardens, but is unarmed and the limp, light green, smooth leaves create a well-furnished bush. A very noticeable character is the width of the stipules. It is not the only American species with this peculiarity and very often the broad stipules are inherited by hybrids of these species. The fragrant flowers are borne in early summer, in large bunches, and create a good effect. They are followed in autumn by plenty of rounded red heps.

It was in cultivation in Britain as early as 1773. The absence of prickles might be expected to have endeared this rose to gardeners' hearts, but there seems to have been little success attendant upon the efforts of hybridists apart from the Boursault roses (see under *Rosa × lheritierana),* if indeed this species was the part-result of that group. *R. blanda* itself is sometimes prickly in nature and the hybrids that have occurred seem to have produced plants with rather poor flowers and as like as not prickles as well. Even so, the possibility of thornless roses is such a boon that it is strange that this character should not be pursued. We only have to think of the ease with which pruning can be done with 'Zéphirine Drouhin' and 'Goldfinch', to say nothing of the Boursaults, to make us wish that this advantage had been striven for in place perhaps of other characters and colours.

89%

Rosa blanda

For too long this rose has been a rarity and uncommon in gardens – it has so many assets. But it is extremely strong growing, achieving at least 6m (20ft) on warm walls, and its pairs of hooked prickles make it difficult to manage. Not that it requires the usual pruning accorded to rambling and climbing roses; it is a very sturdy, yet somewhat lax shrub which makes some sort of support necessary. When the main shoots are trained up, huge annual growth comes forward, downy yet prickly and clothed in highly attractive, prolific leaves, with 7-9 rounded, dark green, glossy leaflets. It is therefore not a rose for small gardens; moreover it will only thrive and produce its flowers in warm situations.

The substantial pure white flowers appear from July until the autumn. When fully expanded during the warmth of the day, they reveal a sumptuous coronal of yellow stamens – only eclipsed, according to E. A. Bowles, by the similar display in the heart of a Japanese anemone. They are borne singly or in small clusters and have a rich lemony scent. Its long flowering period and the great beauty of all its parts has certainly endeared this rose to those who garden in warm climates, and it has become naturalized in parts of the southern United States of America. No mere blackberry could become a more troublesome weed!

It is called the Macartney rose in honour of Lord Macartney's Embassy to the Emperor Qianlong of China between 1792 and 1794. Sir George Staunton, a physician, was included in the Embassy and he and others gathered dried specimens of plants, also seeds; among them were some of *Rosa bracteata* which were given to Kew. When in bud and seed the extraordinary, foliaceous, prickly yet downy bracts can best be seen. The hep is clearly shown in Parsons' painting, which reveals its size and unusual appearance. Parsons also illustrated its double-flowered hybrid with *R. laevigata*, 'Marie Leonida', which opens its flowers well only in hot, dry weather, but the most famous hybrid is 'Mermaid', whose large, single, pale yellow flowers appear over an equally long period on warm walls, accompanied by equally grasping prickles and good foliage. It was raised in 1918 by William Paul of Cheshunt, with a yellow Tea rose as its other parent; it is unfortunately sterile.

Rosa bracteata

Named in honour of Robert Brown, a Scottish botanist who circumnavigated Australia in 1801-03, and later became Keeper of Botany in the British Museum, London. It is a variable species of the Synstylae section (see under *Rosa arvensis*) which has been introduced from several regions around the south and east of the Himalayas – Nepal, Yunnan and West Sichuan. Some of the species in this section have been accorded botanical status such as *R. moschata* var. *nepalensis*, but over so large an area it is inevitable that geographical forms should occur. It is on the whole a slightly tender species in Britain, long young shoots dying back at the extremities after a hard winter. But there is no doubt about its beauty and, apart from *R. setigera*, the sole member of the Synstylae section in North America, it has, in its best forms, the largest flowers in the section. They are pure white, borne in large and small clusters on the long arching branches – sometimes exceeding 6m (20ft) in a season – with a far-carrying fragrance. In some forms the leaves are green, in others of a greyish tint, but at all times long, limp, and inclined to droop; when young, at the end of the long new shoots they are often purplish. It is of extreme beauty in all ways, one of the most noted forms being named 'La Mortola' after the garden of Sir Thomas Hanbury near Ventimiglia, in the north of Italy. A plant of this used to grow at Kiftsgate Court in Gloucestershire; another, in the 1920s, had ascended pine trees to the height of some 12m (40ft) in the University Botanic Garden, Cambridge.

The botanists have long played ducks and drakes with this magnificent species. It was first described in 1820 and thenceforth until about 1880 it was accorded its rightful name of *R. brunonii*. From then onwards until well into this century it was labelled *R. moschata* in botanic gardens, and as such I first knew it. However, the great gardener-botanist E. A. Bowles distinguished the two and about 1960 I obtained cuttings from his plant of *R. moschata*, which is of course totally distinct botanically in leaf and flower. In addition, whereas *R. brunonii* flowers in one overpowering flush at midsummer, *R. moschata* comes into flower later and continues for many weeks. (See also under *R. arvensis*.)

Rosa brunonii

This semi-double form of *Rosa californica* had been known in gardens for many years, but it seemed to disappear from British gardens after the First World War. The plant now grown was purchased from Messrs Bobbink & Atkins of New Jersey shortly after the Second World War by Mrs Ruby Fleischmann, who grew so many old garden roses at Chetwode Manor, Buckinghamshire. Lambertus C. Bobbink had at that time one of the most comprehensive collections of old and species roses in the United States. The painting is an exact portrayal of the plant now grown, though some doubts have been heard about its identity; botanically it conforms exactly to the early detailed descriptions.

It has become a popular garden rose of tall growth, often to 2.7m (9ft), gracefully spraying outwards with a plentitude of fresh green foliage and of flowers. They appear for several weeks and are delicately scented. A fine example may be seen at Hidcote.

There is no doubt that this is a beautiful and showy rose for the garden. However, it takes up considerable space, particularly since it spreads by suckers if on its own roots. In spite of this thorny problem, who, having once seen it in full flower, could have the heart to curtail it? And should this become necessary, there would be no difficulty in finding recipients! There are times when it is obviously a boon to have such suckering roses on a non-suckering rootstock.

As its name suggests, the species is a native of California; from the south of the State it extends northwards into Oregon.

83%

Rosa californica 'Plena'

ROSE 'CALOCARPA'

(*Rosa rugosa* × *R. chinensis*)

It is unfortunate that so noteworthy a rose as *Rosa rugosa* should not find a place in these pages; the specimen selected for Parsons to paint does not appear to me to be a typical form. So we are limited to this excellent hybrid, and, to represent the fruits, the painting of *R. macrophylla* × *R. rugosa*.

'Calocarpa' shows very little of the China rose in its characters; from the name 'Common China Rose', which it is claimed was in the parentage, we may presume that the 'Old Blush China' was used, itself a hybrid as described. The cross was made by Monsieur Georges Bruant of Poitiers, France, and sent out about 1891. Bruant also raised 'Madame Georges Bruant' (1887) and 'Belle Poitevine' (1894), both hybrids of *R. rugosa*. In fact, until the advent of *R. moyesii* and *R. hugonis* in the early 1900s, little interest was taken by the gardening world in rose species apart from *R. rugosa* and *R. pimpinellifolia*. One reason for its popularity was its receptiveness to hybridizing; others were the undoubted merit for gardeners of its repeat-flowering habit, its crops of great fruits, its hardiness, ease of growth and freedom from disease, and its yellow autumn colour. Fortunately 'Calocarpa' has inherited all these assets. It is indeed a splendid leafy shrub which deserves to be better known.

R. rugosa is a native of the Russian Far East, Korea, Japan and north China, described from a collection from Japan in 1784. Thereafter it seems to have been lost and reintroduced as a new species about 1870. It is said to have been cultivated since AD 1100 in China, where it was much used for the making of pot-pourri. The heps are the most fleshy of all, and quite tasty, and are useful for rose-hep syrup, if available in sufficient quantity.

Two very interesting hybrids of *R. rugosa* are 'Schneezwerg' and 'Martin Frobisher', both continuously in flower through summer and autumn. The first is white; the second is derived from the first and is blush-pink.

Rose Calocarpa

One of the smallest-growing of species roses, and fairly small in leaf and flower, this is described as inhabiting rather dry and open habitats in eastern North America from Maine down to Florida and west to the Prairie States and Texas. But in Britain it should be given part shade to preserve its foliage in a fresh state during the summer.

It is a rather weak twiggy bush, spreading by suckers densely clad in prickly bristles, producing its flowers for several weeks at midsummer, and following them with small round red fruits. It was known at one time as *Rosa humilis.*

It is seldom seen in our gardens. A little treasure of a double form 'Plena', with exquisite flowers, depicted in my book *Shrub Roses of Today,* reached me during the 1950s from Mr and Mrs Wilson Lynes of Taberg, New York State; it opened its flowers best when growing in an unheated glasshouse, otherwise they tended to "ball". Both the single and the double have lingered in our gardens without making much impact, almost certainly because propagation has been by budding instead of by allowing the plants to sucker and spread by underground stolons. However much of a nuisance such habits may be in the garden, it is the only way of inducing some of these unusual roses to stay with us. On the other hand, some of the better-known Gallicas are undoubtedly better when on other rootstocks; this gives them vigour and strong flower stems, and avoids the disadvantage of their spreading through other shrubs or into clumps of peonies, for instance, from which they are almost impossible to extricate. This is a point often forgotten by those who invariably advocate "own-root" roses.

95%

Rosa carolina

In this rose we have true *Rosa centifolia*, but with extraordinary leaves – earning it the name of 'Rose à feuilles de Laitue'. Certainly if one considers the lettuce called 'Continuity', the similarity is apt, both the brown tinting and the puckering – or bullation – being present, especially on the strong young shoots produced after flowering time.

The flowers are not usually quite so large as those of *R. centifolia*, but have the same warm pink colouring, hollow centre and gracious droop, besides the rich scent.

All the true "sports" of *R. centifolia* have a rather lanky open growth and need support. I think the best way of doing this is to provide a framework around them of three stout stakes, connected at the top horizontally by three more stout stakes, about 90cm (3ft) out of the ground. The strong young branches come up through this frame and gracefully arch over it. Since grace is so fundamental to the beauty of *R. centifolia*, no support of a stiff nature should be given to it, but just this initial support to keep the great drooping flowers off the ground. The same applies to a few lax growers in the Gallica section.

'Bullata' is reported to have occurred in Holland and was known in England by 1805. It never ceases to astonish.

Rosa centifolia 'Bullata'

The Crested Moss rose originated about 1820, a direct "sport" from *Rosa centifolia*, and is not a descendant of the Moss rose. It was also known as 'Chapeau de Napoléon', the winged and crested calyces supposedly representing the cockades of the Revolutionary headgear.

There is no doubt that these green crests have endeared this rose to all gardeners ever since it was raised and, like the Moss rose, it has been preserved safely, with reverence and delight. Though the growth, prickles, leaves and the clear pink colouring of the flowers remain the same as those of the parent, the flowers are not quite so large and globular. It is as though, in regarding this and the Moss roses, *R. centifolia* itself was a supreme effort of the genus, never to be repeated in other form.

As recorded under *R. centifolia* 'Muscosa', exact details of the origin of *R. centifolia* are not known, but after much scrutiny and observation and reference to old books Dr Hurst concluded that it might well be the result of the fusing of *R. gallica* and *R. damascena* with an admixture of *R. canina* (through *R. alba*), but that all such crosses happened before the dawn of history. And, be it noted, *R. damascena* here mentioned covers both the Summer and the Autumn Damask roses. Both derive some of their remarkable fragrance from members of the Synstylae section, *R. phoenicia* and *R. moschata* respectively.

93%

Rosa centifolia 'Cristata'

ROSA CENTIFOLIA 'MUSCOSA'

Moss Rose

Rosa centifolia originated towards the closing years of the sixteenth century and was first portrayed by Jacques de Gheyn in 1603. Thereafter its great globular double flower – always nodding and with a recessed centre on account of the shorter central petals – has graced innumerable pictures. It became, until quite recently, the main rose-motif in designs for fabrics and wallpapers. It has been conjectured that it was the result of hybrids between the Summer and Autumn Damask roses to which *R. canina* contributed through *R.× alba*.

The Moss rose is so called because of the moss-like proliferations of stalk and calyx, so well shown by Parsons. The "moss" is soft and glandular and exudes a rich aroma. (This is an important distinguishing characteristic, because the Roman Autumn Damask rose also produced a variety with a display of moss, which in this rose is harsh and even prickly; by hybridization in the late nineteenth century the two roses became interbred.)

R. centifolia 'Muscosa' was first heard of on the Continent at some time prior to 1720 and eventually became a great favourite in Victorian times. The leaves and growth are typical of *R. centifolia,* but the flowers are not usually quite so large. On two occasions they "sported" to white forms; one with a slight blush in the centre on opening is, we believe, 'Shailer's White' of 1788. Once again the blooms are not quite so large as the pink moss and the growth is somewhat weaker.

The occurrence in England in 1807 of a single-flowered "sport" of the Moss rose opened the door to raising plants from seed, and later by hybridization, resulting in Moss roses of white, pink, crimson and purple.

Rosa centifolia Muscosa

Probably on account of their ancient mixed parentage many varieties of roses have "sported" to strange forms. There have been climbing "sports" from dwarfs and vice versa; peculiarities have cropped up in regard to foliage and calyx, and also colouring and size of flower. The present Latin name covers one of the most appealing small-flowered "sports" of *Rosa centifolia*. It is also known as 'Rose de Meaux' and was one of two miniatures introduced to Britain from France in the late eighteenth century, having originated at Meaux, to the east of Paris.

The present rose makes a small bush to about 90cm (3ft), with sturdy growth. Otherwise it is like *R. centifolia* reduced in all its parts, but the flowers instead of being globular are flat, more like those of a Gallica. There is also 'White de Meaux', which is an exact counterpart but has white flowers whose centres are pink.

It is remarkable that we know as much about these old garden forms of roses as we do. Their provenance and derivation is only found here and there in books that are extraordinarily indefinite, but the histories of roses, being great favourites of mankind, have been pieced together by ardent workers and close observers. We owe most of the unravelling of the history of this and other miniature forms of the old European roses to Desmond Clarke, who spent so much energy, interest and time on the 8th edition of Bean's *Trees and Shrubs Hardy in the British Isles*.

Another miniature rose often attributed to *R. centifolia* is 'Parvifolia', or 'Pompon de Bourgogne', Burgundy rose. But this is I feel sure a form of *R. gallica*, on account of its lack of prickles and small pointed leaves, and not of *R. centifolia*, to which it has always been ascribed.

102%

Rosa centifolia pomponia

One of the strange facts about this historic rose is that it often masquerades under names of poetic licence which all really belong to Gallica roses: 'Belle des Jardins', 'La Rubanée', 'Village Maid', 'Cottage Maid', 'Panachée à fleur double', 'Dometil Beccard' and 'Dominic Boccardo' being some of them. Considering it was not introduced to Britain until 1845, from Angers, France, it is remarkable that it has got itself into such confusion.

Though there is no proof – since it has not produced a reverse "sport" – it is usually considered to be a "sport" of *Rosa centifolia*. While having the general characteristics of this old rose, it does not convince me of its origin. Its armature and leaves are not the same, its growth is more self-reliant, but its flowers are certainly not far removed from those of *R. centifolia* except in colour. It produces large heps, unlike *R. centifolia*, but it has the rich typical fragrance and rather nodding blooms. When freshly open its colouring is creamy white, striped with bright pink, fading after a day or two to white with pale lilac-pink stripes.

Striped roses were one of the aberrant forms greatly treasured before hybridization became understood. In fact any abnormality was an asset to a garden where only a handful of roses were grown, mostly pink. Even today the odd striped seedling crops up and is named after some flamboyant personality.

Rosa centifolia Variegata

Rosa chinensis has excelled all other species in producing miniature forms. Here we have a little plant, seldom exceeding 45cm (18in) in height, with good clear colour, form and fragrance, producing flowers out of doors from midsummer until the autumn frosts. No legitimate name has ever been published for it in western botanical books, so that we can scarcely do better than adopt the present one – which was first proposed by Gordon Rowley in the *Journal of the Royal Horticultural Society* in 1959 – as a delightful compliment to Miss Willmott. So far as I can ascertain, Parsons' painting was the first that was ever published of it in Europe, though it seems that it had been in cultivation at Heathfield Nurseries, Welwyn, Hertfordshire, since the China roses were first introduced (Rowley, *ibid*), at the end of the eighteenth century. In recent years I have received identical plants from China, where it has been known as 'Chi Long Han Zhu' (signifying "with a pearl in red dragon's mouth") since the mid-1800s. It has been growing for many years on the rock garden at Wisley.

Another crimson rose arrived, by way of Europe, at about the same time; it grew in the garden of Gilbert Slater at Leytonstone. This was first described in the *Botanical Magazine* in 1794 and was named *R. chinensis semperflorens*, which was the name used by Miss Willmott, and has similarly become known as 'Slater's Crimson China'. It had a larger, looser flower with glandular bristly pedicels, and was of much taller growth than Miss Willmott's. It was evidently not so suited to our climate as Miss Willmott's, but Gordon Rowley obtained plants of a crimson China rose which had been preserved in Bermuda, which proved to be practically identical to *R. chinensis semperflorens*. The Bermuda Rose Society has recently sent cuttings of this rose to me. Dr Hurst did not see this Bermuda rose and confused Miss Willmott's with Slater's and the figure of the latter in the *Botanical Magazine*.

There are two other old crimson Chinas, both single-flowered; 'Miss Lowe' is a small plant like Miss Willmott's. I have had it for many years, having been given cuttings by E. A. Bowles who was a friend of Dr Lowe of Wimbledon. This closely resembles the painting by P. J. Redouté in *Les Roses* of 1817, Volume 1, p.49, as *R. indica*. The other is a sturdy, wide bush which flourishes in the sandy soil at Wisley, having been presented to the garden under the name of 'Bengal Crimson'. (Many of the roses from China were originally known to Europeans as *R. indica*, or Bengal roses, because of their having reached gardens in India prior to being introduced to Europe.) This rose was first listed in my *Manual of Shrub Roses*, 1962, as 'Sanguinea'. It is a worthy garden plant, but little known.

Rosa chinensis

This is one of the great sights from summer to late autumn at Kiftsgate Court, Gloucestershire, where it has been growing for many years, making huge bushes about 2.4 x 2.4m (8 x 8ft). The small, dark foliage is coppery when young. The painting by Parsons does not show all of its colouring; the pointed buds are of vivid orange-flame; on opening the flowers are of soft chamois-yellow; after pollinating they turn to coppery pink, and on the third or fourth day the colour deepens to coppery crimson before they wrinkle and fall. The full range of colours is to be found in the illustration in my *Shrub Roses of Today*. In the height of summer the stout plants are covered with blooms showing all these colours together – a truly remarkable sight. Strong young shoots arise and produce the later flowers.

Nobody knows its origin. In *The Genus Rosa* it is simply called 'Miss Willmott's *indica*' and it is quite likely that it was brought from the south of France, where these slightly tender roses grow so well. The celebrated alpine gardener of Geneva, Henri Correvon, wrote in the *Revue Horticole* for 1934 that it was given to him about 40 years previously by Prince Gilberto Borromeo of the Isola Bella, Lake Maggiore, Italy, where it had made a hedge 2.1m (7ft) high. It reached Britain in 1916 from a nursery at Pallanza, on the same lake. Correvon very suitably called it 'Mutabilis', but he was unfortunately not aware that there was already a *Rosa centifolia* form called 'Unique Blanche' or 'Mutabilis', which has caused some confusion. In a later number of the *Revue Horticole* a correspondent claimed that it derived from the isle of Réunion via Madagascar, which points to a possible Chinese origin. It is pretty certainly of a similar parentage to the four original Chinese roses mentioned under the 'Old Blush China'. It has also been known as 'Tipo Ideale' and *R. turkestanica*; this last possibly indicates that at one time it was considered to be similar to *R. foetida bicolor*, which was known by the old German name of "die Turkische Rose".

It seems strange that so spectacular a plant should not be better known. It would be a wonderful bedding rose for public parks in warm counties and would give more flowers per season than any other rose. On warm sunny walls it may be trained up to 6m (20ft) or more.

Rosa chinensis Mutabilis

The Summer Damask rose's origin is obscure, but Dr Hurst concluded it was a pre-history hybrid between *Rosa gallica* and *R. phoenicea*, the Synstylae rose from Asiatic Turkey, Cyprus, the Lebanon and also parts of Greece. The Damask roses are renowned for their scent and this would be derived from this Synstylae species rather than from *R. gallica*, which, though fragrant, is not markedly so. We shall make further acquaintance with Damask roses later in these notes.

What we may call the ordinary Summer Damask is botanically *R. damascena trigintipetala*. It will reach 2.1m (7ft) in height, less in width; has large and small prickles, small, drooping downy leaves and flowers that for size and colour do not compare with the Gallicas and Centifolias. On the other hand, while *R. gallica officinalis*, the Apothecaries' rose, gave rise to an industry producing dried petals because they were able to retain their fragrance for months, even years, the Damask rose has resulted in a far larger industry in Bulgaria and elsewhere, where the petals are distilled to make rose-water and the very valuable attar of roses. If we bear in mind that about three tons of half-open flowers (over a million) have to be gathered at dawn in order to produce 1.1kg (2½lb) of attar, some idea can be obtained of the scale of operations and the value of attar. Almost 3,000 hectares (over 7,000 acres) are devoted to this crop, and as the flowering period is at most only about three weeks, it is a national effort to secure the harvest at the crucial time, at the end of May.

Sometimes our present rose is called *R. damascena rubrotincta*, but it is obviously a hybrid and not a true Damask rose. Nothing is known of its origin, but it was listed by William Paul, the famous nurseryman of Cheshunt, Hertfordshire, in 1888. Other fanciful names include 'Margined Hip' or 'Reine Blanche', but I think nobody will dispute the beauty of this rose, whose poise and colouring have been so faithfully reproduced by Alfred Parsons.

Rosa damascena 'Hebe's Lip'

A beautiful garden shrub with few prickles, achieving about 1.8m (6ft) high and wide; it can also be trained as a semi-climber to greater height. Its origin is something of a mystery. Monsieur Dupont, a famous Paris nurseryman who died in 1817, and who created a noted collection of roses in the Luxembourg Garden in Paris, named it *Rosa nivea*, but Lindley named it R. 'Dupontii' in 1825 and was under the impression that it had been raised from *R. moschata*. Its leaves are downy beneath and this downiness could be inherited in part from the Damask rose, *R. damascena*.

Alfred Parsons' painting captures its beauty well. On opening the flowers are of creamy pink, fading to nearly white in hot weather. To pass by a bush in full flower at midsummer is to savour in full the delicious fragrance which is wafted "free on the air", as Sir Francis Bacon put it. This free-flowering scent is another characteristic of the Synstylae section, to which *R. moschata* belongs. The heps are oval, red, but not borne freely. Its great value in the garden is in its cool colour scheme, the foliage being pale and assorting well with the delicate blush of the flowers.

90%

Rose `Dupontii

It will be noted through these pages that the brightest of the yellow species roses are all native to what we vaguely call the Middle East – Turkey, Iran, etc. – and also to Afghanistan; now this species extends into Pakistan. As we go farther east the colour pales, and farther west there are no yellow species. No doubt some eminent scientist could offer a reason. And botanists have decreed that they all belong to one section, the Pimpinellifoliae, which includes the Burnet or Scotch roses.

Parsons' painting accurately shows *Rosa ecae*, but Miss Willmott called it *R. xanthina*, by which name it was first known. It was discovered by Dr Aitchison in 1880; his wife's initials were E.C.A. and hence the species' name. With so beautiful and well drawn a portrait as Parsons' there is no need for me to add much in the way of description, but the broad-based prickles, absence of thorns or bristles, and leaves slightly fragrant from the glands on their under-surfaces, are all characters distinguishing it from allied species such as *R. xanthina*. The small flowers of brilliant buttercup-yellow are just what is needed as a full contrast to one of the spring flowering, evergreen ceanothuses. And fortunately both plants thrive in hot sunny positions in the garden. It will achieve 1.5m (5ft) or more, but is always a plant of rather thin upright growth.

Two good garden hybrids of recent origin are 'Golden Chersonese' and 'Helen Knight', both of which retain the bright colouring and small leaves. 'Helen Knight' was raised from open-pollinated flowers, probably crossed with a form of *R. pimpinellifolia*; the other was a cross with 'Canary Bird', which is a representative of *R. xanthina* in our gardens.

My particular favourite among the yellow rose species is *R. primula*. It takes its name from its primrose-yellow colouring. It makes a large bush covered in somewhat sticky foliage, which sheds a far-carrying aroma of incense on warm days.

Rosa ecae

Botanizing in what is now Soviet Central Asia, Madame Olga Fedtschenko discovered this species in 1878; she sent it to the Botanic Garden at St Petersburg (Leningrad); thence it was sent to Warley and from the plant there Parsons made his painting. I think this is the plant I have always known, and which thrives at Wallington, Northumberland, in the border devoted to plants with white or pale flowers and grey foliage. This brings home at once its value in the garden.

A vigorous bush, ascending to about 2.4m (8ft), it spreads by means of suckers. In their first season these suckers with their luxuriant, very pale grey-green leaves are contrasted by masses of pink bristles and prickles. The whole bush is well covered in grey-green leaves, among which the pure white flowers appear freely at midsummer. What is more, every new small or large shoot of the summer produces blooms from the main flush on towards autumn. It is therefore a useful shrub for the more spacious or wilder gardens, where it can spread by means of its suckers, and give a distant, cool effect. And to complete the picture, the flowers result in small, bright red heps.

Relatives of this rose, with grey-green leaves and white flowers, are *Rosa beggeriana* from central and south-western Asia, and *R. murieliae* from western China. The first has foliage redolent of the Sweet Brier, but their flowers, like those of *R. fedtschenkoana*, have an unpleasant heavy scent like that of *R. foetida*. While *R. beggeriana* grows to much the same size as *R. fedtschenkoana*, *R. murieliae* gets much larger, even on the gravelly soil at Kew. Muriel was the name of the daughter of E. H. Wilson, its discoverer.

86%

Rosa fedtschenkoana

It is not surprising that this rose, so prolific in its flowering, has been a popular garden plant since its raising by one of the same name in France in 1857 or earlier. If pruned hard every year in early spring it will make a compact short plant of about 90cm (3ft), but if allowed to go its own way it can be classed as a shrub rose, achieving 2.4m (8ft), albeit somewhat spindly.

The small and large clusters of flowers make a splendid show from midsummer onwards, opening large and richly coloured on really good soil, as depicted, but fading to lighter tones with age and on poorer soils. It has a clean, sweet fragrance reminiscent of sweet peas. I have seen it looking particularly pleasing when planted with *Rosa glauca (R. rubrifolia)* with a foreground of *Salvia officinalis* 'Purpurascens', both of which have purplish foliage, toning well with the soft colour of 'Fellenberg'. At one time, in France, it was known as 'La Belle Marseillaise'. I have been unable to find out where M. Fellenberg had his rose garden; perhaps it was at Marseilles.

We do not know its parentage, but it has always been classed as a Noisette, which indicates that the Musk rose and the China rose may be concerned. The term Noisette commemorates two brothers of that name. One, Philippe, living in Charlestown, South Carolina, was given seeds by John Champney of the same town, who had raised a hybrid between the Musk rose and 'Parsons' Pink' China rose. This was called 'Champney's Pink Cluster'. Seeds of this were sent to Philippe's brother in Paris, Louis Noisette, and produced a plant of repeat-flowering habit known as 'Blush Noisette', which is still frequently seen in old gardens. It is very prolific in flower and can reach some 3m (10ft) in height.

92%

Rose Fellenberg

ROSA FOETIDA

The Austrian Brier

Here we have an enigmatic rose over the provenance and origin of which few botanists agree. I think it is now settled, however, that the name of *Rosa lutea* gives way to *R. foetida*, and that it is considered to be a native of Russian Central Asia. Like many other plants it no doubt spread by commerce into western districts and has been found, probably as an escape from cultivation, as far away as the south of France. It is small wonder that it should have "travelled" in this way because it is of a far brighter, more sulphurous yellow than any other known rose and spreads, though only slowly, by suckers. Since the sixteenth century it has been called the Austrian Brier, no doubt from its chance occurrence in that country. It has been treasured in cultivation in Europe since the sixteenth century, and was brought to England by Sir Henry Willock in 1838.

It is unique in many ways. The rich brown young wood turns to grey in the third season. The foliage is a bright, rich, parsley-green with coarse serrations, which make a wonderful foil for the dazzling flowers, whose odour – I will not call it fragrance – is heavy and unpleasant. It seldom bears fruit in cultivation and is usually sterile – which, of course, could indicate a hybrid nature.

In gardens it is rather gaunt and open in habit and resents being pruned; it is far better to let it interlace and form its own shape without attention. The best bushes I have seen are growing in the open; if trained on a wall it does its best to grow away from it, and away also from any shade from trees or shrubs. Unfortunately its blooms are very fleeting and there is no repeat of the display, but few plants of any kind can compete with its brilliant colour.

Rosa foetida

ROSA FOETIDA 'BICOLOR'

Austrian Copper Brier

Without doubt this is the most spectacular rose known, its astonishing colour having caused its preservation by gardeners since its first observance in the Arab world in the twelfth century or earlier. Its name of Austrian Brier or Austrian Copper simply refers to its having been first recorded as coming from that country.

With the same twigs and foliage of the parent species, the same odour and other characteristics, it suddenly bursts upon the June scene – or even earlier – with its astonishing nasturtium-red colour, made the more brilliant by the yellow tint of the backs of the petals. It sometimes "sports" back to the original sulphur of *Rosa foetida* itself; then it may be said to be by far the brightest thing in the garden – for a few days, perhaps a week or more. It is best to plant it well away from all the old French roses and indeed the majority of species which are of some shade of pink.

The double yellow form of *R. foetida*, the Persian Yellow, is a rose of equal growth and character to *R. foetida*. Presumably growers tired of roses in European cultivation bearing nothing but flowers of white, pink, mauve and maroon, because Pernet-Ducher, a rose nurseryman at Lyons in France, spent many fruitless years in trying to hybridize the double Persian Yellow with various Hybrid Perpetuals, eventually succeeding at the end of the nineteenth century. The result was the beginning of our brilliant yellow roses of today and also the two-toned roses of some shade of pink or red backed with cream or yellow, a character inherited from the Austrian Copper. While there are some six or eight pale or bright yellow wild species of roses native to Asia, none had really entered into the strain of modern roses apart from the pale yellow of *R. gigantea*. It was therefore left to *R. foetida* and its forms to change, totally, the coloration of the European rose hybrids early in this century to an ever more strident range of tints, helped by the spontaneous occurrence of a new colour, pelargonidin, which cropped up during the 1920s. It is said that this brilliant rose from Asia also brought with it the "black spot" disease, which we do not read about until this century.

Rosa foetida 'Bicolor'

This is presumed to be a hybrid between *Rosa banksiae* and *R. laevigata,* and was brought from south-eastern China in 1845 by Robert Fortune, together with 'Fortune's Double Yellow'. It is a climbing rose of considerable vigour, but except in the most favoured situations does not flower freely in Britain. The comparatively large flowers, when freely produced, certainly make good effect but they are of a strangely greenish white and cannot compete with other purer white ramblers. As with the Banksian roses, the strong shoots should be allowed to grow and branch to encourage blooms off the smaller twigs.

Our gardens were enormously enriched during the nineteenth century by the several ancient Chinese hybrid roses, which had for so long been esteemed in their gardens. It was a case of ancient, treasured roses of our Western civilization meeting with their counterparts from the Far East; each had something to give the other in colour, shape, fragrance, foliage or season of flowering. We are apt to forget that the most superlatively formal roses of France, derived from *R. gallica* and its relatives, were raised after the advent of the roses from China. The European strain went on being developed and "fancied" while gradually hybrids occurred with the Chinese roses which later altered the whole progress of the genus towards our modern roses.

90%

Rosa x fortuneana

A tender climbing rose, once-flowering, but when once seen in full flower it is unforgettable. It was my good fortune to see it covered with bloom in an unheated greenhouse at St Catherine's, Leixlip, County Kildare, Ireland, in May. The multicoloured fragrant blooms were open in their hundreds. It grows on a sheltered wall at Mount Usher in County Wicklow, but does not flower so well there out of doors. It certainly needs a warm and dry climate to give of its best.

It was introduced by Robert Fortune in 1845 to Standish & Noble's nursery at Sunningdale, having been found "in a rich Mandarin's garden at Ningpo", on the coast of the province of Chekiang, China. For some years its flower production was inhibited by winter or spring pruning, but as soon as it was understood that it should only be pruned (as for all once-flowering roses) immediately after flowering, all was well.

It will be seen from the above that it has only just lingered in cultivation, and yet there must be many favoured climates where it would thrive on a sunny wall and give a spectacular display every year, achieving at least 6m (20ft).

Its origin is unknown but it is undoubtedly yet another of the ancient Chinese hybrids between *Rosa chinensis* and *R. gigantea*, and from both parents it would receive vigour. The fact that it only flowers once is supported by the fact that when strong climbing species are crossed and produce dwarf bushy plants they tend to be repeat-flowering. This has retained its vigorous, climbing growth and therefore does not share in this repeat-flowering character. I only hope that the publicity being given to this remarkable and brilliant rose here may result in renewed interest in it. We certainly cannot afford to neglect it.

Rose 'Fortune's Double Yellow'

This species, cultivated before history began, is the grandparent of all the roses grown and treasured in the cradle of our civilization in Europe: the Gallicas themselves, the Damask roses, the Centifolias and the Albas. And its influence is found in hybrids with several other species as well. It is found wild with little variation from southern and central Europe away east to the Ukraine, Asia Minor, the Caucasus and Iraq. It is a suckering shrub seldom ascending to more than 1.2m (4ft), with few prickles of any size; rounded, rather rough leaflets and glandular flower stalks and calyces which leave a warm aroma on the fingers. This special character is inherited by its derivations. The heps are rounded, red and quite conspicuous.

Of the two forms depicted by Parsons, our normal garden form seems most nearly approached by that which Miss Willmott called *Rosa gallica* var. *austriaca*, but a rose with such wide distribution and so long treasured as a cultivated plant is bound to exhibit considerable variation. Parsons' drawing of *R. gallica* itself shows an extra petal or two to the normal five.

Because plants were treasured for their uses long before their beauty, this rose outbid all others on account of its special ability to retain its sweet fragrance in its petals after drying. Its splendid semi-double form *R. gallica officinalis* is reputed to have been brought from the Near East by the Crusaders in 1239–40. This form would have been more treasured than the single for the simple reason it provided more petals for drying, apart from its flamboyant beauty. Its size, as against *R. gallica* itself, can be seen by comparing the portrait of this rose with *R. gallica* 'Versicolor'. Because it was used so much for conserves and medicines, it became known as the Apothecaries' rose. A great industry was born at Provins, in France, to meet demand in Europe and also with considerable export to the West Indies. For this reason it is also known as the rose of Provins, which has caused confusion with the Provence rose, *R. centifolia*. A similar industry was carried on in Mitcham, Surrey. Besides its officinal qualities *R. gallica*, and in particular *officinalis*, was raised by seed especially in Holland; the Dutch from early days were to the fore in Europe in raising, selecting and distributing all manner of plants because of their beauty. *R. gallica officinalis* is also reputed to be the Red Rose of Lancaster and to have given rise to the regular form of the rose of heraldry. The first Earl of Lancaster married the widow of Henri I, King of Navarre, whose emblem was this rose.

105%

Rosa gallica

'Rosa Mundi' is a well-known name for this remarkable "sport" of *Rosa gallica officinalis*, whose flowers are of the normal light crimson or dark pink of the latter, with much of the petal-area being a blush-white, variously striped and spotted. It is unfortunate that Parsons' painting shows the two tints with less marked distinction between them than is usual. This form was first recorded in 1665, but nothing more is known about it. It has been associated, conjecturally, with Henry II's mistress, the Fair Rosamund.

As a garden plant up to some 1.2m (4ft) on good soil it is spectacular, equally as vigorous as its parent, equally as floriferous and fragrant, and bearing the same rounded red heps. Both types are apt to contract mildew on the soft new shoots of late summer.

While 'Rosa Mundi' frequently reverts to *R. gallica officinalis*, I have never noted a fresh, spontaneous occurrence of the striped form. It is important to remove any red-flowered shoots at the time of flowering, or they will gradually take over from the striped form. Apart from *R. rugosa*, these Gallica roses are the only ones to which shears can be taken in winter to keep them in the form of a hedge, if desired.

This striped rose is often called 'York and Lancaster', but it is quite distinct from this variety of the Damask rose (*R. damascena versicolor*) which is a lanky, prickly, downy-leafed bush up to 1.8m (6ft) or more, and carries smaller, rather flimsy flowers of pale pink more or less particoloured (not striped) with white.

'Versicolor' is just as good for pot-pourri and preserves as the typical *R. gallica officinalis*, about which the future Louis XIII, aged fourteen, wrote to his father Henri IV, in 1605: "Papa, all the apothecaries of Provins have come to me to beg me to ask you, very humbly, to give my company a different garrison-post, because my *gendarmes* like the *conserve de roses* and I am afraid they will eat it all and I shall have none left. I eat some every night when I go to bed ...".

Rosa gallica 'Versicolor'

Rosa gallica is unique among the roses of the western Old World to have forms which are of dark vinous crimson, even leaning towards maroon and purple. Otherwise this place in the spectrum is held by *R. chinensis* and *R. moyesii*, but the latter has not taken a general part in the breeding of modern roses. The purplish colouring of the European strain of roses was much prized for most of the nineteenth century, until towards the end of the century the soft yellows and salmon pinks of the Tea roses focused the eyes on a different set of tints (to be superseded in this century by the dazzling hues which resulted from bringing *R. foetida* into bearing).

Parsons' picture of this rose is quite wrongly entitled *R. provincialis*, which is a synonym for *R. centifolia*; evidently Miss Willmott did not grow the true *R. centifolia*, because under this name Parsons gave us a portrait of yet another false rose and no relation to the Moss rose.

Our present rose is undoubtedly closely related to *R. gallica*, but may perhaps have some other rose in its parentage, for it will achieve 2.1m (7ft) in height, a lanky rather sprawling shrub, quite unlike *R. gallica* except in the size of its leaves, the absence of any but quite small prickles and the depth of colouring of the fragrant blooms. I believe it to be the same as 'La Belle Sultane', 'Maheka' and perhaps 'Cumberland', all of which are likely to be very old. It has one splendid display at midsummer. If it can be trained through a big, single pink Gallica derivative such as 'Complicata', or 'Andersonii', the intense crimson which quickly becomes flushed and veined with purple will be the more appreciated and the growth supported.

101%

Rosa gallica Violacea

It is said that this extraordinarily vigorous rose, with the largest flowers in the genus, is not hardy in Britain. It is a native of north-eastern India, Upper Burma and Yunnan, and over its areas of distribution varies considerably from near white to palest yellow in flower, from about 8.5cm (3½in) wide to at least 12.5cm (5in). It is the largest pale yellow type which is here depicted by Parsons, and which used to thrive in the Cambridge University Botanic Garden glasshouse in the late 1920s. I had not again seen this superb form until I found it growing and flowering freely in 1970 on the pergola at Mount Stewart in Northern Ireland, where it had been planted by Lady Londonderry. The property is now owned by the National Trust; the old plant died for no apparent reason, but had been propagated and distributed. It is a gracious rose with long, limp, satiny leaves; there is a pencil drawing of it in my *Gardens of the National Trust*, sketched at Mount Stewart.

At some far distant time this rose and *Rosa chinensis* var. *spontanea* had come together in China and the ensuing hybrids had been growing as garden plants – although roses are not over-popular in China – and thence the four main hybrids reached Europe as recorded under the 'Old Blush China'. It is presumably *R. gigantea* from which the repeat-flowering habit was mainly derived; certain it is that the great convoluted petals, inbred through countless generations of hybrid roses, gave rise to the long-petalled shapely buds of the Tea roses, which are so tantalizingly beautiful. Tantalizing because they are not quite hardy enough for our climate. The pale yellow also was a new colour and cropped up again and again through the late-nineteenth-century Tea-hybrids, the only instances of this colouring until after 1900, for which see under *R. foetida* 'Bicolor'.

R. gigantea has to its credit the first yellow hybrid climbing roses, known as the Tea-Noisettes, the oldest that we still grow being the fruity scented 'Desprez à fleur jaune' of 1830. 'Céline Forestier' and 'Gloire de Dijon' followed it, culminating in 'Maréchal Niel' in 1864. This in effect might be described as a double form of *R. gigantea* of enriched yellow colouring, though it was of course a hybrid. The great, drooping flowers with scrolled petals are of unequalled beauty in their way. In hot weather they open to perfection at Mottisfont, Hampshire. They can also be grown under glass.

The other great character that we owe to *R. gigantea* is its fragrance. It is exactly like that of a freshly opened packet of tea, and this has been transmitted to many of its hybrids, giving rise to the term Tea rose.

Rosa gigantea

A rose which is much better known under its synonym: *Rosa rubrifolia*; it is also known, less aptly, as *R. ferruginea*. Its two first names both call attention to the colour of its leaves, which scarcely resembles the tint of any plant other than some sedums and sempervivums. For us gardeners there is no doubt of the value and beauty of the plant, so we can leave the botanists to fight it out between the names (to which may be added *R. rubicunda*).

It has long been known as a native of the mountain ranges of Europe from the Pyrenees to the Carpathians and farther south to Yugoslavia and Albania. There is scarcely any necessity for me to call attention to its clear pink, white-eyed flowers, so well depicted by Parsons, but it is as well to recall that by September another display is laid before us: that of the brownish-red oval to spherical heps. The flowers are fleeting but the fruits are showy for about two months. It makes a good shrub; the young shoots are of glaucous or purplish colouring, the strongest wood having prickles, but it is not an unmanageable – or unmannerly – plant. In gardens it is usually about 2.1m (7ft) high and wide, but among other shrubs it will often grow taller. As a rule it can be raised from seed with little variation, but occasionally a hybrid will crop up. One such is 'Carmenetta', a hybrid with *R. rugosa*, which has added vigour and prickles but little else.

In full sunshine the foliage is richly coloured with coppery purple; in shade it is a light glaucous green, or pale jade colour. While, therefore, in sun it is a good shrub for a warm rich colour scheme, it is perhaps doubly valuable in shade, since there are so few grey-leafed shrubs which give of their best in those conditions.

R. × redoutea is a hybrid that crops up from time to time between *R. glauca* and *R. pimpinellifolia*. It was named for P. J. Redouté by Thory in their great joint work *Les Roses* in 1817 as *R. × redoutea glauca*. It used to be catalogued by Leslie Slinger at the Slieve Donard Nursery, County Down, in the early 1960s under the name of *R. rubrifolia alba*. It has some of the glaucousness of the foliage of *R. glauca*, but flowers of blush-white edged with pink, and a suckering habit. It has recently been retrieved from oblivion by Dr E. C. Nelson in Ireland.

Rosa glauca

This remarkable hybrid was raised between *Rosa persica* and *R. clinophylla* about 1830 and has just lingered in cultivation since, but is seldom seen and is usually short-lived. I am not sure whether it has proved short-lived from cuttings as well as from grafts. It used to grow successfully against a sunny wall in the University Botanic Garden, Cambridge, reaching to about 90cm (3ft) in height and width, but the most successful that has been recorded was a plant at Berkeley Castle, Avon, where it was more than twice this size.

It is considerably more showy than its parent *R. persica* (q.v.), and it will be noted that the leaves have three lobes and stipules, unlike *R. persica*. The hep, also, has few prickles. Otherwise the influence of the other parent, *R. clinophylla*, is not much in evidence. This is a rather tender rose, related to *R. bracteata* and a similarly vigorous grower. Unfortunately it is not at present in cultivation, though it was introduced around 1803 and was still observed in 1834. It should be noted that this rose is native to riversides and similarly wet places, which are seldom colonized by roses. Moreover, what successes have been recorded of the cultivation of *R. × hardii* have not been due to moisture, but rather to sun and quick drainage, which is what we should accord to *R. persica* itself.

Natural hybrids have been observed in the wild in Russia and also in Iran, and hybrids with several cultivars have been made in this country by J. L. Harkness, but these proved sterile. The original cross was raised by J. A. Hardy, Curator of the Luxembourg Garden, Paris. It is a pleasant thought that both Monsieur and Madame Hardy are commemorated in plants raised by J. A. Hardy – *R. × hardii* and the splendid white hybrid Damask rose 'Madame Hardy'. This last is not likely to go out of cultivation, but we shall have to look to *R. × hardii*, in case it should be in danger of neglect. Meanwhile, success has in part been achieved by Jack Harkness in putting on the market in 1985 a low, spreading, thorny bush, bearing small leaves with five segments, and semi-double flowers of clear yellow with a marked red eye, about 2.5cm (1in) across. It flowers at midsummer, with a few later. It is called 'Tigris' and is *R. persica* × 'Trier'. Other hybrids are on the way. One day he will breed one which is fertile and then we may find that *R. persica* has started a new dynasty of rose hybrids, in the same way that *R. foetida* did nearly a hundred years ago.

83%

Rosa x hardii

For us today, surrounded by hundreds of varieties of garden roses both yellow and double, it must seem difficult to realize that this was the only double yellow rose known, from its discovery in the early seventeenth century to 1838 when the Persian Yellow was brought into cultivation, and then again until early in this century when bright yellow hybrids were raised. And our present rose was not even a good garden plant, for this country at least, whatever success it may have had in France. (For we should not forget that the French have ever been to the fore in raising roses – supposed to be so English.) Except in warm dry weather, on a bush well ripened by sunshine, it must generally be considered a failure, though it grows well enough in gravelly soil at Mottisfont and in suitable seasons regales us with those full globular flowers so often painted by the Flemish painters as counterparts to the pink *Rosa centifolia*. On account of its size of globular flower, it was often described as the Yellow Provence Rose or Sulphur Rose.

It is no doubt a very old rose, judging by its prevalence in gardens of the Middle East. It is here, too, that the single-flowered counterpart, its type species *R. rapinii* grows. I have never seen it, but its foliage is grey beneath, as is that of *R. hemisphaerica*. This bears fruits of orange or yellow colouring and it would be a useful rose to reintroduce. It differs from *R. foetida* in having hooked prickles and the greyish foliage, and also in possessing a sweet scent, but it is obvious that the two roses are related and both are of historic importance apart from their colour.

People went to great trouble to grow *R. hemisphaerica* to their satisfaction, in some cases double-working it, which means budding it on to a rose which has already been budded on to a rootstock. But all to no avail; we must, I think, accept that this rose is as intractable in our ordinary garden conditions as are the species of iris and tulip from the same part of the world. Maybe it would thrive better in a dry-aired glasshouse, which is where the best blooms of the Tea rose 'Maréchal Niel' are consistently produced.

Rosa hemisphaerica

A natural hybrid reputed to be between the Dog rose (*Rosa canina*) and the Burnet or Scotch rose (*R. pimpinellifolia*), though the resulting progeny which we know shows little influence of the latter. Its parentage is in doubt; it may be a local form of *R. canina* or of some other species native to Ireland. The large sepals projecting from the rounded, or very broadly ovate heps make it obviously different from *R. canina* itself.

It was found in 1795 near Holywood in County Down, a few miles north-east of Belfast, by John Templeton. He fortunately propagated it and sent some plants to the National Botanic Garden at Glasnevin, Dublin. Here it was named *R. hibernica*, the Irish rose. At one time the original plant in Ulster had spread through suckering roots over a large area, but road-widening and other activities during the last hundred years or so found its stock very decreased. It was first given to me by Lady Moore, about 1955, though I have lost it since. Lady Moore was the wife of Sir Frederick Moore, Keeper of the National Botanic Garden at Glasnevin. The last remaining plant was taken to Belfast in the early 1960s, where it still grows in the garden of the Department of Botany in Queen's University.

The Irish rose used to have a very long flowering season; in one instance the record was from May to November, though no doubt flowers were few and far between after its summer flush.

Rosa x hibernica

Although even as far back as the eighteenth century, shrubs of foreign origin were used to decorate the fringes of copses and landscapes, their appraisal really started in Victorian times in Britain, when shrubberies became a vogue as important as summer bedding. Even so the shrubby species of roses were seldom included apart from a few Burnet roses, Sweet Brier and *Rosa rugosa* towards the end of the century. To be taken to heart more fully rose species needed a fillip, and this they received in the early years of this century by the introduction of *R. hugonis* and *R. moyesii*, two of the most spectacular of species, and indeed of a brilliance and beauty to compete successfully with most other shrubs. Only the most phlegmatic mortal could fail to be impressed by either of them. And they are also satisfactory garden plants for our climate.

Seeds were sent to Kew by Father Hugh Scallon from Shensi Province in the north-west of China; they flowered in 1905, when the plant was described, and these same plants still survive at Kew and flower well after more than three quarters of a century in the same spot on shallow, gravelly soil. This speaks wonderfully for their constitution; unfortunately plants propagated by budding are not so healthy. They should be grown from cuttings.

The luxuriant foliage, giving the plants a feathery appearance, often turns to a purplish tone in autumn, when by careful searching the small maroon-coloured heps may be seen. In Parsons' picture the prickles are distinct and in evidence, but in addition to such armature some plants (of wild provenance from later collectors) show wide winged prickles not unlike those of *R. sericea pteracantha*, though not so brightly coloured. It is thought that the original plant known as 'Hidcote Gold' may have been one of these. Otherwise the most important hybrids of *R. hugonis* are undoubtedly 'Cantabrigiensis' and 'Headleyensis'. Both of these are of good growth when budded on understocks, the former of fairly narrow upright growth to 2.7m (9ft), and the latter equally high and wide.

R. hugonis is sweetly scented; the flowers seldom open more than Parsons shows, often remaining in cup-formation.

87%

Rosa hugonis

Although this rose is seldom seen in gardens, I have included it because its parents *Rosa wichuraiana* × *R. rugosa* have had much influence among garden roses raised in this century. There must be few species of rose with which *R. rugosa* has not hybridized; this cross was made in the Arnold Arboretum in the United States by Jackson Dawson towards the end of the nineteenth century. It reached Kew in 1897. It is a hardy, shrubby, graceful bush to some 2.4m (8ft) in height and width. The cross was again made in Connecticut in 1919 and a selected clone was named 'Max Graf'. This is a hardy, semi-prostrate shrub much used for ground-cover; being dense and prickly it will not only smother weeds but keeps dogs and other small animals at bay.

It so happened that Wilhelm Kordes, the famous German rose breeder, ever trying to raise roses that would stand the cold winters of central Europe, obtained this hybrid with an aim to using it in his breeding programme. But, while *R. rugosa* has been so ready to hybridize, its progeny have always been sterile. Presumably this was what Kordes was hoping to overcome – and he was rewarded. For under his care two heps were at last produced from many attempts at crossing, and one of the resulting two seedlings proved to be fertile. It had, in genetical parlance, doubled its chromosomes and was in effect a new species. It was named *R. kordesii* in 1951 and became the parent of a race of new hardy climbing roses with large flowers. Among them are the well-known 'Leverkusen', 'Dortmund', 'Hamburger Phoenix' and 'Parkdirektor Riggers'. The two Japanese species, therefore, apart from their own intrinsic values, have been to the fore in the breeding of climbing roses.

Rosa x jacksonii

If we were to assess the merits of all the species of roses native to Britain, I think the Sweet Brier would stand first. The fragrance of the foliage alone gives it a high place among plants which give of their scent freely upon the air, about which Sir Francis Bacon was so keen. Then there are its quite enchanting flowers, of a warmer pink than those of the Dog rose, and also deliciously fragrant. And in autumn it can hold its own with any rose for its display of heps. They may not be so large as some, but their glittering abundance and scarlet colour are arresting. It makes a vigorous bush up to some 2.7m (9ft) and is terribly prickly; even this can be turned into an asset if one is plagued by trespassers! Today it is usually called *Rosa eglanteria*, a tribute to its old vernacular name Eglantine, but this name has often exchanged places with *rubiginosa*, and its forms and hybrids may be found under either. It is a native of Europe and northern Africa.

The subject of this note is a spectacular flowering rose which the Reverend C. Wolley-Dod is reported to have found in a Cheshire lane, far from gardens, but it is obviously a hybrid. The Cheshunt nursery of William Paul listed it in 1892. If, as is suggested, it is a hybrid of the Damask rose, it has fortunately preserved some of the Sweet Brier's fragrant foliage, but it does not bear heps. It does not do, however, to be greedy, and with a plant such as 'Janet's Pride' producing its display of unique flowers once a year we should be satisfied. The continuity of flowering of so many modern roses has made us expect so much from a rose, though we are content with the single display of the majority of our garden delights.

Rose 'Janet's Pride'

ROSA LAEVIGATA

Cherokee Rose

It may seem strange that a rose native to China should be adopted as the State flower for Georgia in the United States of America. Yet such is the prolificity of this vigorous climbing rose that it has become more or less naturalized in that State, where it has earned the name of Cherokee rose, after the native people. There is no record of when it first was brought to America; it is reported to have flowered there by 1803, whereas its flowering in Britain is recorded in 1825. Previously information came that it was growing in the Chelsea Physic Garden in 1759.

The painting at once shows it to be a rose of no ordinary beauty. In the first place its handsome glossy foliage has only three lobes instead of the usual five or seven. Next, its large flowers are supported by pedicels well covered in bristles, which extend to the incipient hep and the calyx lobes. It thrives best in warm climates; the only plant I have lately seen is on the house front at Endsleigh in Devon. I had it at one time but, like *Rosa gigantea*, it succumbed to a severe winter. Being nearly evergreen it is a beautiful plant when out of flower.

No doubt its tenderness prevented *R. laevigata* from being used much as a parent for hybridizing, but its large and sumptuous flowers seem to have been given to 'Anemone' and *R. × fortuneana*. It is sweetly scented.

Rosa laevigata

The other name for this hybrid is *Rosa × reclinata*, a hybrid which had been raised by the French nurseryman Vilmorin in 1912, and recorded by Thory in the Redouté classic. He also recorded a rose of the same presumed parentage between *R. chinensis* and *R. pendulina*. But modern cytology refutes this parentage, *R. blanda* (an American species in cultivation in Europe since the late eighteenth century) being preferred to *R. pendulina*. Whatever may be the facts, this cross gave rise to a small group of hybrids called Boursault roses, after a keen grower of roses in Paris towards the end of the eighteenth century. Their lack of fragrance is balanced by their total lack of armature; they flower very early in the season and are strong-growing climbers. Their colouring – pink, and one purplish crimson – was a welcome addition to the handful of garden ramblers at that time. Today they are almost forgotten, which is a pity because nothing quite measures up to the early charm of 'Blush Boursault', 1848, and 'Madame de Sancy de Parabère', 1845. The flower drawn by Parsons seems to me to resemble most closely the former; the latter's flowers are characterized by extra-large outer petals. They both have large showy flowers. Considerably smaller is 'Amadis', 1829, which has fully double flowers of crimson-purple with an occasional white fleck or stripe, which is not unusual in hybrids of *R. chinensis* of darker colouring. Both this and 'Madame de Sancy de Parabère' are represented in colour in my *Climbing Roses Old and New*.

Another Boursault rose, 'Morletii', not raised until 1883, is more of a shrub, with smooth arching branches of purplish crimson; the unfolding foliage in the spring is of reddish brown, and it dies off in autumn with good bright colour. At midsummer the stems are well set with medium-sized, purplish pink flowers. It should be pruned annually by removing two- and three-year-old stems from the base, which will create a fountain-like display of blossom. It has also been known erroneously as *R. pendulina* 'Plena', and achieves at least 1.5 x 1.5m (5 x 5ft). It is a rose of many attributes and grows well at Hidcote, Gloucestershire.

94%

Rosa x lheritierana

A vigorous sprawling rose which is as good for trailing down a bank as it is for covering a stump, broken tree or hedgerow; or it will climb into a low tree if the main shoots are trained up. Left to itself it will make a mound about 1.5m (5ft) high and 3m (10ft) across, but will climb, with help, to 3–3.6m (10–12ft). There is no doubt it is one of the most beautiful of large-flowered single roses; from pink buds the flowers open to a delicate cream-pink, fading to blush-white as they age. They cover the long trailing branches and have a pronounced, sweet fragrance. The stems are thorny, the leaves dark green, of neat outline and make a good background for the pale flowers, which are followed by rounded red heps.

It is no doubt a hybrid of *Rosa gallica,* but there is no record of its raising; it was grown at Bitton Vicarage by Canon Ellacombe in 1888. It has been confused with another rose, the authentic *R. macrantha* which was described as early as 1823, but which seems no longer to be in cultivation.

A similar rose with a few extra petals is 'Daisy Hill', raised prior to 1906 by T. Smith of Daisy Hill Nursery, County Down, but it is not so vigorous. It has an advantage over 'Macrantha' in wet weather, since the flowers tend to remain open; this slight failing in 'Macrantha' is also noticed if sprays are taken indoors – they close by the evening. 'Daisy Hill' has a claim to later fame in being one of the parents of 'Raubritter', raised in 1936 by Wilhelm Kordes. This is a much smaller plant when left to sprawl on its own, but can be trained into small trees to a height of 3m (10ft); its flowers are scentless, pink, semi-double and globular, each one lasting for at least a week.

Rose Macrantha

This is probably the tallest and largest of the shrubby rose species except *Rosa moyesii*. But it has a much more graceful habit than *R. moyesii*, the great prickly stems arching and weeping over, the whole perhaps 4.5m (15ft) high and wide. It is when the shrub is fully established that its great beauty is revealed, for the flowers, up to 7.5cm (3in) across, of warm deep rose-pink, nod down at a charming angle, often poised at and above eye-level. Many plants can be grown in its ferny shade because it does not usually make bushy growth at the base of the stems.

And then again in late summer and early autumn the long, oval to flagon-shaped heps hang down, singly and in small bunches, bright red and conspicuous. While the heps are bristly and the great basal shoots have big prickles, the shrub is not unduly armed on the red-brown twigs. The leaves are not the largest in the genus – an honour reserved for *R. sinowilsonii* – but are composed of five to eleven leaflets, and may be as much as 20cm (8in) long. The flowers are scarcely scented.

This species has a wide distribution from Kashmir and Nepal through the Himalayas to western China. It has been in cultivation since about 1818. More recently introductions have been made by George Forrest from north-west Yunnan in 1917, and two forms have been named 'Rubricaulis' and 'Glaucescens' by Hillier & Sons of Winchester. The former is noted for the purplish colouring of the young stems, bracts and receptacles, and the latter for the glaucous colouring of the young stems and leaves. In 1954 from Nepal came a specially large-fruited form named by Maurice Mason for his son, 'Master Hugh'.

Another large-fruited rose probably owes its splendour to *R. macrophylla* – 'Doncasteri', raised between the wars at J. Burrell & Co.'s Cambridge nursery. 'Auguste Roussel' was raised by Barbier at Orléans, France, a cross between *R. macrophylla* and 'Papa Gontier', a Tea rose. The result is a graceful medium-sized shrub of arching habit and shapely semi-double flowers of clear light pink.

87%

Rosa macrophylla

Although this is an unnamed rose, and the actual plant from which the painting was done is probably no longer in existence, I feel its great beauty deserves inclusion. This is partly because *Rosa rugosa*, with large globular fruits, and *R. macrophylla*, with flagon-shaped fruits, both retain the dead calyx lobes which give the heps so much character, and also because *R. rugosa* so readily hybridizes with other roses that such crosses frequently have been raised. The two roses are in the same Cinnamomeae section of the genus.

Looking at the hybrid depicted, we see the profuse prickles of *R. rugosa* and foliage midway between the two species. The heps show a shape approaching the globular of *R. rugosa* but with the neck and forward-projecting calyx lobes of *R. macrophylla*. Miss Willmott gave no description nor origin of this rose, which is certainly a good example of what the Cinnamomeae can achieve. *R. moyesii* and its relatives have fruits of similar shape; even so, in spite of the fame of this species for its long flagon-shaped fruits, such a hybrid as this could well hold its own for spectacular effect. It is an indication of what the genus *Rosa* can do in the late summer and early autumn, early enough for them to be considered as candidates for special colour schemes for that season. Many other kinds keep their red fruits into late autumn and winter, the most spectacular and long-lasting being 'Scarlet Fire' raised by Wilhelm Kordes; it is as brilliant in fruit as it is in its midsummer glory of single scarlet flowers. The full range of shapes and sizes of rose fruits is shown in an illustration in my *Shrub Roses of Today*.

Rosa macrophylla x R. rugosa

ROSA MAJALIS

R. CINNAMOMEA 'PLENA'
Cinnamon or May Rose

Although I have been trying to detect a smell of cinnamon from flowers or leaves of this rose for about forty years, I have been totally unsuccessful, though my nose is well trained! Desmond Clarke, with whom I worked on roses for Volume IV of *Trees and Shrubs Hardy in the British Isles* by W. J. Bean, 8th edition, suggests the term may apply to the soft brown of the bark.

This, the double form of the single pink species, has long been known in gardens, John Gerard having described it in his *Herball* of 1597. Because of its early flowering it was referred to as the Rose de Mai, Rose du Saint Sacrement and Rose de Pâques; hence the name of *Rosa majalis*. The Parsons painting shows a double form of really delightful clear pink; forms that have come my way have been smaller and of purplish pink. It is one of the earliest recorded double forms of roses, and Mrs Gore in her *The Rose Fancier's Manual* of 1838 states that it is a favourite in all gardens. This makes me think that she must have known the form depicted by Parsons. It makes a somewhat sparse and twiggy bush of about 1.2m x 90cm (4 x 3ft) and is perfectly hardy.

The single-flowered type is considerably more vigorous, up to 1.8m (6ft) at least, and as beautiful in its flowering and fresh green leafage as any other species; it bears more resemblance to the several American species of the Cinnamomeae section – rather than to the Asiatic species which include such disparate individuals as *R. rugosa* and *R. moyesii* – having, indeed, the wide stipules so prevalent in the Americans. It is a native of central and northern Europe and Siberia.

Rosa majalis

This is the yard-stick against which the larger species roses are measured. Apart from *Rosa rugosa* and *R. pimpinellifolia*, gardeners took little interest in the wild roses of any country for garden furnishing before the end of the nineteenth century. Upon the gradually growing interest in flowering shrubs burst this astonishing plant, shown in 1908 by Messrs Veitch. It had been seen in western Sichuan in 1893, but was introduced in 1903 by E. H. Wilson.

It is a great, often gaunt, shrub reaching 3m (10ft) in height; good specimens of the original introduction grow at Nymans, Sussex. The lower parts of the strong new shoots are heavily armed with spines and prickles, which are much less in evidence on the flowering shoots. The painting shows well the glorious colouring of the flowers, and also the tints of the stems, stipules and calyces. Wonderful though the floral display is, as with so many single-flowered roses, it is of short duration; on the contrary by August there starts a display lasting for two months or more of the splendid large, scarlet, bottle-shaped heps.

It is a strange fact that if this red-flowered type of *R. moyesii* is raised from its own seed, as like as not the resulting shrubs will have pink flowers. In nature both colours are found. The botanists have long been in two (or more) minds about the nomenclature of this pink type, but it is generally referred to as *R. moyesii* var. *fargesii* or *R.m.* 'Fargesii', though apparently there is nothing to indicate that the Abbé Farges had anything to do with its discovery. Two names that crop up for pink *moyesii* are *R. moyesii rosea* and *R. holodonta*, but these should apply to the nearly related species *R. davidii elongata*.

From a garden artistry point of view these pink *moyesii* forms are a little difficult to place; totally different colour-scheming is needed for the flowers and for the fruits.

Brian Mulligan, then Assistant to the Director at Wisley, selected two splendid forms which had been raised in that garden prior to 1937. The most brilliant is 'Geranium' which, in addition to a particularly dazzling colour of flower, is a more bushy and compact plant than the original *R. moyesii*, with lighter-coloured and more plentiful foliage. The other is 'Sealing Wax'. Both are noted for their large bright heps. In almost every instance, for brilliant flower and hep I should choose 'Geranium' for planting in gardens.

90%

Rosa moyesii

Introduced to European cultivation between 1860 and 1875, from the Far East, where it is a native of Japan and Korea, this rose has had a great influence on the hybridizing of garden roses. It is yet another of the Synstylae section (see under *Rosa arvensis*) with free, arching growth of long, overlapping slender shoots, small leaves and extremely abundant single creamy-white flowers, borne usually in large trusses. Various forms have been selected during this century, some for their thornlessness – a useful character, because it was at one time much used as an understock for propagation by budding.

The nurserymen Cress and Danieli of the United States raised a form which they named after themselves, and compared with all the forms I have seen, it is the most beautiful in flower, though selected for its suitability for budding.

Free-flowering forms present an unforgettable sight with far-flowing intense fragrance. This fragrance is usually transmitted to its offspring, but a more constant character to look for is the laciniation of the stipules – in other words, the leaf-like flanges at the bottom of the leaf stalk are fringed. Some well-known old ramblers with this characteristic are the pale pink 'Blush Rambler' of 1903 and 'Goldfinch' of 1907, warm yellow fading to almost white, both of them deliciously fragrant. Good forms of *R. multiflora* itself are of considerable garden value, when grown on their own as graceful arching bushes, or when allowed to ramble over hedgerows or into small trees. In autumn they come into their second beauty, the multitudinous flowers having produced an equally prolific show of tiny red heps. And yet another asset has been discovered in the United States, where, on account of its dense, arching but bushy growth and ease of cultivation, it is used to prevent soil erosion and as a crash-barrier on motorways. Its heps provide nourishment for birds.
Truly a rose of many parts!

In addition to being used as a parent for ramblers, *R. multiflora* has given rise when crossed with China roses, to dwarf "sports". These, the Dwarf Polyanthas, are reliably repeat-flowering and gave rise, in their turn, to the Floribundas.

Rosa multiflora

Those who admire the wild species roses but have only very small gardens would do well to consider this little plant. As it has been in cultivation since 1807, it is surprising that a plant with so many merits is not better known. Apart from other considerations it excels in its brilliant autumn leaf-colour, in common with two other species from North America – *Rosa virginiana* and *R. foliolosa*.

I have never seen it higher than about 60cm (2ft), its red-brown stems so densely covered in prickly bristles that they look like plush – but do not feel like it! These bristles are also red-brown and give it a special attraction in winter. The erect stems bear many quite small, narrow leaflets of glistening dark green, which adds to colourfulness in autumn. The brilliance of the scented flowers is not exaggerated in the Parsons picture, but we are looking at a representation of the original introduction. Unfortunately it has sometimes been raised from seed and there are several hybrids in gardens; one is a much coarser plant and is known as 'Alburyensis'. The small red heps of the species are hispid.

These little roses are at a disadvantage in many gardens, where, when species are considered, a plant of at least 1.8m (6ft) is usually in mind. However, like some forms of *R. pimpinellifolia, R. virginiana, R. carolina* and others, they will make dense, suckering thickets which are just right for the outskirts of the heath garden, larger rock garden or semi-woodland. There they can spread as they wish and will not be cursed.

Rosa nitida

A rose of great antiquity, having been depicted on silk in AD 1000 in China. Between 1792 and 1824 four hybrid roses reached Europe from China: 'Slater's Crimson', a tender rose of crimson colouring, which still grows in Bermuda; 'Parsons' Pink', which is our present rose; 'Hume's Blush', which I hear of also in Bermuda, and 'Parks' Yellow'. It was these repeat-flowering but rather tender roses which were used so much during the nineteenth century in France and in England to alter the trend of rose selection from the old European groups related to the Gallica roses. The new "blood" had a profound effect, first producing what became known as the Bourbon rose, and later the Hybrid Perpetuals. By dint of deliberate hybridizing with 'Hume's Blush' and 'Parks' Yellow', the Hybrid Teas were developed.

The four Chinese hybrids were derived over countless centuries in that country, between *Rosa chinensis* var. *spontanea* and *R. gigantea*. In the wild both of these are of lax or semi-climbing habit; their four progeny were bushes and repeat-flowering. This last character was inherited from *R. gigantea*, with its long shapely petals. *R. chinensis* var. *spontanea* grows in Hupeh in western China; it was discovered by Dr Augustine Henry in 1885 but has never been introduced to Europe. I have seen coloured photographs of it showing a large scrambling shrub with single flowers from pale pink to dark crimson, deepening with age.

'Old Blush China' (Common Blush or Monthly Rose) is therefore a valuable hybrid, which, with its relatives, has had a profound effect on our garden roses. It is hardy in England and has long been a favourite. It is considered to be the "Last Rose of Summer" of Thomas Moore, and well it may be, because it continues to flower until frosts stop it. In California it has produced a climbing form. It is constantly in flower through the summer and was a favourite with Gertrude Jekyll for its continuity and cool pink colouring. She used it in the great parterre at Hestercombe, Somerset, though when the Lutyens design was replanted of late years, for some unknown reason the similar 'Nathalie Nypels' was used.

It is believed that Sir Joseph Banks introduced 'Old Blush China' in 1789 and it is recorded that it flowered first in the garden of a Mr Parsons at Rickmansworth, Hertfordshire. Being certainly a hybrid of ancient lineage it is wrong to call it the China rose, a name which belongs to the wild type of *R. chinensis* called var. *spontanea*, which as yet has never been introduced to Western gardens.

Rose 'Old Blush China'

Recorded in all the Floras of Alpine Europe, the native alpine rose has long been a favourite, partly because of the almost complete absence of prickles or thorns. It is a comparatively small-growing, suckering bush with reddish or purplish stems, usually growing to about 1.5m (5ft). The leaves are aromatic, smooth and thin. The attractive flowers are produced very early in the rose season and are followed by flagon-shaped heps, like those of *Rosa moyesii* but much smaller; they are sometimes smooth, sometimes bristly, but all are finished with a narrow neck and persistent calyces.

In spite of ease of growing and of handling, it is seldom seen in gardens – presumably because its blooms are fleeting. One of its synonyms is *R. pyrenaica,* but just to confuse things a small growing form has been known for over fifty years as *R. pendulina* 'Pyrenaica' or 'Nana'. Clarence Elliott records that he received this from Arthur Clutton Brock, but its origin is not recorded. Like the type species it spreads freely by suckers and there was a large colony of it in A. T. Johnson's garden in the 1950s, scarcely exceeding 30cm (1ft) in height. The richly coloured flowers are followed by bristly red fruits. It seems that dwarf forms are prevalent in the Pyrenees, for one was recorded as early as 1885.

R. pendulina was long considered to be one of the parents of the Boursault roses (see under *R.* × *lheritierana*).

It is worth recording here that the Alpenrose of Europe is in reality *Rhododendron ferrugineum.*

Rosa pendulina

At first sight few people would recognize this as a rose. The principal difficulty of identification would be the single leaf, with no basal stipules, characters not found in any other species. The colouring of the flowers would also be confounding. And yet, examination of the bud and the heps would leave little doubt in the mind.

Rosa persica is a unique species, native to Iran, Afghanistan and south-east Russia; the plants from the more eastern regions are glabrous, whereas those from Iran and Afghanistan have leaves covered in fine down. It is a small suckering shrub in nature, up to 90cm (3ft) in height and armed with short prickles. The flowers are borne singly and open in early summer, with a prickly calyx tube which develops into a rounded prickly hep.

Apparently it is so common in certain districts that it is dried for fuel. It has been grown from time to time in this country: it is recorded as having been kept alive for more than twenty years in an unheated greenhouse at Kew, planted in loam and mortar rubble, and shaded. The place where I first saw it growing out of doors was at Highdown, Sussex, on raised beds in full sun in that warm, sheltered garden. Here it was on its own roots – having been raised from seed – and though only a few inches high, it was in flower and spreading freely. I obtained some scions for grafting; these were successful and I hoped that by planting them deeply they would make roots of their own, but all gradually failed. Plants were given to Wisley and Kew but without the desired results. It has been reintroduced of late years and has grown well from seeds; several hybrids were raised by J. L. Harkness but all proved to be sterile. The original plants have thrived in a scarcely heated glasshouse and have made good bushes. (For further notes see under *R. × hardii*.)

Owing to its odd characters this species has been given separate generic rank, under the name of *Hultheimia berberifolia*. It has also been known as *R. berberifolia* and *Lowea berberifolia*, but here at least it stays under *R. persica*. It was introduced first from Persia (Iran) about 1790.

91%

Rosa persica

There are innumerable forms of the Scotch or Burnet rose, *Rosa pimpinellifolia* (*R. spinosissima*) in gardens; not only do they spread freely by suckers and so make distribution easy, but they can be raised readily from seed, great variation in colouring being found. There are about a dozen recognized double-flowered garden forms from the dwarf plum-coloured 'William III' to the tall double white. One that is established by pictures and descriptions in old books is 'Andrewsii': it was named in honour of Henry C. Andrews whose rare and valuable old book, *Roses*, of 1805-28, occasionally comes on the market. Though there are many pink forms to be seen in gardens in Britain, very few have the clarity of tint found in 'Andrewsii', which in some lights has a hint of salmon. Miss Willmott recalls that it is common in French gardens.

The Scotch rose and its forms in white, pink and purplish colouring are extremely hardy and are able to fend for themselves and increase by underground stolons even in the sand on the sea shore. In fact, sea shores are where they are likely to be found round our coasts, and from Iceland to eastern Siberia and south to the Caucasus and Armenia. In pure sand they may be only a few inches high and a hazard for bathers' bare feet, but many forms in the garden will ascend to 1.5m (5ft), especially the delectable double white. They all flower once, early in the season, and have a fresh and delicious fragrance. In the autumn the heps appear, almost black and the size of a large black currant, at which time the foliage takes on dusky purplish hues or may turn to orange. They may have just five petals to the flowers or may be double with 25 or more, of one tint, or mottled and variegated, sometimes with a much paler colour on the satiny backs of the petals compared with their matt upper surface. Their charm is perennial and all-pervading.

Long before the beginnings of modern roses in the nineteenth century, forms of Scotch or Burnet roses reached a great height of popularity in Britain, over two hundred forms being listed by a Scottish nurseryman; in 1848 William Paul of Cheshunt was offering 76, all with fancy names and descriptions of two or three words only. It is impossible to relate these names truthfully to garden forms today.

It will be noted that yellow Burnet roses have a less pleasant fragrance than those of other colours and it is supposed that they are all hybrids of *R. foetida*, both singles and doubles, such as 'Lutea Maxima', *R. × harisonii* and 'Williams' Double Yellow'.

Rosa pimpinellifolia Andrewsii

Miss Willmott states that the sample from which the picture was made came from her garden at Tresserve, in the south of France. Possibly this accounts for the smallness of the flowers; they may have opened too quickly in the spring warmth. It is well known under the name of *Rosa pimpinellifolia* var. *altaica*, but according to botanical minutiae, this rose should have innumerable bristles (like those of *R.p.* 'Hispida'), whereas our present plant has mainly small prickles. *R.p.* 'Grandiflora' makes a vigorous bush up to about 1.5m (5ft), spreading very freely by its own suckers, so much as to be a nuisance in some gardens where it has insufficient space. It is far removed from the usual forms of Scotch rose.

It can, moreover, prove equally vigorous in almost any soil, even in chalk as at Highdown, Sussex. Its foliage turns to a purplish tint in autumn and its heps are few but large and of maroon tint; its flowers are quickly over. Any resolve to get rid of it entirely, made in winter when one has to dig out its roots wandering far and wide, is broken as soon as its arching branches are again covered with the 7.5cm (3in) wide, gracious, fragrant flowers.

Wilhelm Kordes used it in Germany, where it is perfectly hardy, to produce a series of superlative hybrid roses such as the semi-double yellow 'Frühlingsgold', single ivory-white 'Frühlingsanfang', and pink 'Frühlingsmorgen', all of which have become established favourites and are richly scented. It is also a parent of the double white 'Karl Foerster'.

R.p. 'Grandiflora' has been in our gardens since its introduction from Siberia before 1820.

93%

Rosa pimpinellifolia 'Grandiflora'

Considering that *Rosa pimpinellifolia* has myriads of thorns in any case, this name may not be particularly evocative. This is a rose very seldom seen, but once seen it is not easily forgotten. The prickles and thorns are long, sharp and straight, and of dark colour, contrasting strongly with the pale flowers.

Botanically it is distinct from the variable *R. pimpinellifolia* (*R. spinosissima*) the Scotch or Burnet rose, in that its leaves are often doubly toothed (not shown in the drawing), while their undersurfaces, the flower and leaf stalks, stipules, pedicels and sepals – in other words all the young growth except the upper surface of the leaves – are covered in fragrant glands.

I have not found var. *myriacantha* to be anything like so vigorous either under or above ground as other forms of the Scotch rose. It is from the more southerly distribution of the species and has been found in southern France, whence it was named in 1805. It is worth searching for afresh, and should be in our main rose collections. It seldom exceeds 1.2m (4ft).

It often amuses me, when contemplating working among prickly rose bushes, how much we should welcome a range of roses without armature. Against this convenience is the fact that the shape and size of prickles or thorns are certainly as much help in distinguishing rose species as all their other characters.

88%

Rosa pimpinellifolia var. myriacantha

The Burr or Chestnut rose, *Rosa roxburghii,* is so called because of its large green heps which are covered with stiff prickles. It is a big thrusting shrub about 3m (10ft) high and wide, armed with pairs of forward-pointing prickles and noticeably greyish bark, peeling like paper off old branches. There is no rose like it. The foliage, too, is distinctive, being composed of 9-17 small leaflets which accounts for its synonym of *microphylla.* The flowers are single, from white to pink in its wild state in western Sichuan, China. E. H. Wilson introduced the single pink form in the early years of this century and it is this type which is usually seen in gardens. Beautiful wide flowers, they are pale pink, modest and slightly nodding, with a sweet, fresh scent.

It is unfortunate that the double form, which is here depicted, is by no means as hardy nor as vigorous as the single type. Unlike the wild single type, which is known as *R. roxburghii* (*R. roxburghii normalis* or *R. microphylla*), the double form is an ancient Chinese garden form. It reached us from the Calcutta Botanic Garden and first flowered in Colvill's nursery at Chelsea in 1824.

I have had the double form more than once and for some years it grew well at Hidcote, but usually died to ground-level in winter. This is sad because not only are the double pink flowers very beautiful, but they are produced intermittently from summer until autumn in a warm season. Parsons' painting does not reveal the full beauty of the open flower in which the outer petals are much larger and paler than those bunched in the centre, at which moment the flower resembles the form of a double hollyhock.

It has been used a few times for hybridizing, but the older hybrids are almost non-existent; among them are 'Jardin de la Croix' and 'Triomphe de la Guillotière'. A hybrid raised by Dr C. C. Hurst is 'Coryana', possibly crossed with *R. macrophylla;* it flowered in 1926. It is a fine, large, leafy shrub with single dark pink flowers rather hidden by the copious foliage.

Uniting with *R. rugosa* it has produced a valuable shrub *R. × micrugosa;* Dr Hurst raised a second generation among which was a white-flowered plant 'Alba', which is repeat-flowering and highly desirable.

Rosa roxburghii 'Roxburghii'

ROSA SEMPERVIRENS

The Evergreen Rose

A native of southern Europe or northern Africa, and occasionally found in an apparently wild state in southern England. It is seldom seen in gardens but belongs to the same Synstylae section as *Rosa arvensis*, from which it may at once be distinguished by its shining, almost evergreen leaves. The long trailing shoots are green, the single white flowers, sweetly scented, being borne in clusters in the axils of the leaves as in all the species of this section. It has not been used for hybridizing, but a few old spontaneous hybrids occurred in the garden of the Duc d'Orléans, raised by the head gardener A. A. Jacques, at the Château Neuilly, near Paris. The best-known of his seedlings, raised in 1826 and 1827, are 'Adélaïde d'Orléans' and 'Félicité Perpétue'.

It is strange that neither of these is notable for its scent, which is negligible, unlike 'Splendens' (for which see under *R. arvensis*). On the other hand they are free growers and very hardy, with semi-evergreen leaves; they make a thick tangle of slender branches suitable for training over arches and hedges and into small trees, which they will transform into a bower of creamy blossoms at midsummer. Before the advent of the numerous rambling roses descended from *R. multiflora* and *R. wichuraiana*, they were of considerable garden value and may be seen in photographs in *Roses for English Gardens* written by Gertrude Jekyll, 1902.

Rambler roses are not in great favour today, having been neglected for large-flowered climbers, but there is no gainsaying their prolificity and grace, unsurpassed by any other plants.

Rosa sempervirens

ROSA SERICEA

(R. OMEIENSIS)

A unique species in that it has usually only four petals; it is also unique in one of its forms for the very large colourful prickles. It has a wide distribution in nature, including Nepal, north-eastern India, the Himalayas, south-eastern Tibet, north Burma and western and central China, and as a consequence introductions from the different regions show considerable diversity. In all however one thing is constant, the neat small leaves divide into as many as eight pairs. This gives the plants a ferny appearance whether the bushes be 1.8 or 3.6m (6 or 12ft) high and wide.

The sweetly scented flowers are carried singly and make a good effect in late spring or early summer and are followed by small rounded heps in late summer. Sometimes the pedicel of the hep is thickened and colourful in red or yellow. So far as is known these forms occur only in certain Chinese districts. One with yellow heps has been called 'Chrysocarpa'; another, without prickles or thorns, 'Denudata'; 'Polyphylla' was a name given to a form with numerous leaflets.

But the two most noted forms are *Rosa sericea pteracantha* and 'Heather Muir'. Although the species had been known since 1822, it had not made much headway in gardens; white- or cream-flowering species of rose were not much appreciated. But interest was awakened in 1905 when George Paul of Cheshunt showed stems of *R. sericea pteracantha* at one of the Royal Horticultural Shows, obtaining for it a First Class Certificate on account of the wide scarlet prickles. This form when severely pruned is highly spectacular in late summer when the strong new shoots are made conspicuous by this remarkable armature. 'Heather Muir', on the other hand, lacks this ornamentation. It was obtained by the then owner of Kiftsgate Court, Gloucestershire, from George Bunyard & Sons and has always been a splendid large shrub with a long flowering period. The flowers are cream, followed by orange-red heps on thickened stalks of the same colour. 'Hidcote Gold' has five-petalled flowers of clear yellow – probably from *R. hugonis* – and some of the wide winged prickles of *R. sericea pteracantha*. Botanically this should be referred to as *R. × pteragonis*, and the same applies to 'Earldomensis'. I suspect that 'Cantabrigiensis' owes some of its vigour and elegance to *R. sericea*, the other parent being probably *R. hugonis*, but we are entering into difficulties here, because forms of *R. sericea* from the wild have also been known to have yellow petals.

87%

Rosa sericea

The Synstylae section of the genus has been discussed under *Rosa arvensis*. The species extend from southern Europe and northern Africa right away to Nepal, China, Japan and Korea, with just this one species in North America, where it is known as the Prairie Rose. It occurs from Ontario to Florida and west to Kansas and Texas – a varied array of climates and conditions, and from what I can hear it varies considerably in colour and form, which is not surprising. In Britain it is represented by the form drawn so well by Parsons; it is a big leafy bush of arching habit, with wide flowers of mid-pink. There are usually only three leaflets. It is very far removed from the European and Asiatic Synstylae roses in every way, except for the tell-tale uniting of the styles. It is my belief that the free-flowing fragrance of the other species emanates from the stamens, not from the petals; *R. setigera* is sweetly scented, in spite of what is written in many books, but not overpoweringly fragrant as in its relatives.

One of its assets as a species is that it flowers after the main mass, with *R. wichuraiana, R. davidii* and *R. multibracteata*; another asset is that practically thornless forms have been found. It seems to me that the potentialities of this species – which, I am told, vary from white through pink to crimson – have not yet been made available to our gardens. Perhaps these notes may prompt some keen spirit to investigate. So far it has only inspired two hybridists and the results are seldom seen. Among them are 'Baltimore Belle' and 'Long John Silver'. A trap for the unwary is the fact that a botanical synonym for *R. setigera* is *R. rubifolia*, the blackberry-leafed rose, not to be confused with *R. rubrifolia*, for which see under *R. glauca*.

R. setigera is unique, I believe, among rose species in that its stock in the wild spreads much by self-layering shoot-tips, as if it were a *Rubus* species. As seedlings differ in their sexes, being dioecious, Roy Shepherd has pointed out that quite large groups of one type occur in the wild as a consequence. Prolific vegetative reproduction often goes hand-in-hand with limitation of seed-production, witness the English elm and Ground elder.

Rosa setigera

Making a very large bush with masses of interlacing, arching shoots, this rose is suitable for the wilder parts of the garden, if only because its numerous hooked prickles make it unmanageable. Fortunately it has several assets which outweigh its disadvantages. The foliage is small and of a distinctly greyish hue, making a delightful picture at flowering time and again in autumn when the hundreds of small orange-coloured heps ripen. In bud the small flowers are yellow, opening to milky white, borne in small and large clusters. Like the several other species of the Synstylae section, its fragrance is strong and free on the air. In spite of the unusual colouring of the foliage and its other assets, it has rarely been used as a parent for hybridizing. It was crossed at Kew with the red-flowered rambler 'Hiawatha'; the result is 'Kew Rambler' which has single pink flowers and has inherited some of the greyness of the foliage. This is a pleasing, fragrant rambler.

It is a native of Sichuan, western China, and is named after the French Jesuit missionary, Father Soulié, one of many of that calling who did so much to bring to the notice of European gardens the riches of the Far East. It will achieve some 3m (10ft) in height and as much through, and there is no doubt that the soft colouring of the leaves and pale flowers give it much value in accentuating distance when planting a large area. Although on the whole it is hardy in England, its long new shoots sometimes die back in a hard winter.

89%

Rosa soulieana

So far as scanty records relate, this was a self-sown seedling rose found in a garden or hedgerow in Stanwell, Middlesex, and was propagated and put on the market by the famous nurseryman Lee of Hammersmith in 1838. Considering that nothing like it has been raised since, and that it has so many merits, it is very fortunate that it received this attention all those years ago, and that it remains a good, vigorous bush. Parsons' painting was obviously done from a well-nurtured specimen, though as a rule the petals are smaller but in greater quantity.

It makes an arching, sprawling bush of about 1.5 x 1.5m (5 x 5ft) and is the better for some support, such as a frame of wood around it, or it will cascade happily down a bank. The bluish-green of the leaves tones perfectly with the silvery pink of the flowers, which are produced continuously from June until autumn and have a delicious fragrance.

Obviously related to the Scotch or Burnet rose, *Rosa pimpinellifolia* (*R. spinosissima*), in order to account for its perpetual flowering habit it is generally thought that its other parent might well be the old Roman Autumn Damask rose. In the 1830s the only other repeat-flowering roses with which it could have hybridized were *R. moschata*, *R. chinensis* hybrids and the Portland rose. The first two give no indication of their presence in 'Stanwell Perpetual' and the latter is, of course, derived from the Autumn Damask rose.

This is a rose that needs looking at again and again, to impress on ourselves that in it we have a very wonderful garden plant – a present from Dame Nature of great beauty and fragrance.

Rose 'Stanwell Perpetual'

One of the very few roses that usually bears leaves of only three segments. Apart from that it is a strange-looking rose with wiry, branching twigs set with occasional thin sharp thorns or narrow prickles and also thickly covered with microscopic starry down, which gives it its name. The heps and calyx lobes are also prickly and the hep is open at the top, but has persistent sepals. It comes from the United States, ranging from west Texas to Arizona. It overlaps with *Rosa stellata mirifica* in New Mexico. The flowers are produced over a long period during the summer and have a soft, silky texture, like those of a *Cistus*, with creamy yellow stamens.

I do not think *R. stellata* is still in cultivation in Britain. It was first collected in the Organ Mountains towards the end of the last century and has not been quite so amenable to cultivation in our gardens as its variety *mirifica*.

This variety is quite hardy and from a garden point of view is very similar; though the green twigs are also covered in down, it is not stellate and though the leaves sometimes have only three leaflets, they more often have five which is usual in roses. It is therefore not quite such a delightful trap for the less knowledgeable visitor! I have known this to achieve 1.5m (5ft) in height even in the shade of a wall though both of them do best in hot sunshine. It is found within the same area as *R. stellata*, but apparently limited to the Sacramento Mountains, whence it was introduced in 1917. In nature it is said to cover areas many acres in extent and must be a most unpleasant, almost impenetrable thicket, for it spreads by suckers as well as by seeds. This little rose, in flower or not, excites more interest than any other shrub in my garden, having been taken for a gooseberry by more than one "expert". Another close relative is *R. minutifolia*, but this does not seem to be as hardy as the above two kinds.

Rosa stellata

It could not be claimed that the American species of roses compare favourably with the great variation in size and colour of the roses of the Old World, but in this species we have a rose of many and varied assets. It is very hardy, makes a thicket of red-brown twigs and branches, spreading by suckers if on its own roots. The thicket is quite conspicuous in the winter sunlight. The leaves are glossy, rich green and provide good autumn colour from orange to red. The flowers are borne late in the season, of bright clear cerise-pink and are followed by long-lasting round red heps. It withstands wind better than most roses. By turning to Parsons' picture we can see what quality it has in flower, but cannot detect the fresh fragrance. No doubt it varies in colour considerably in its native habitat, which extends from Newfoundland to Pennsylvania. The plant depicted and described is an old introduction to Europe, in perhaps the early part of the eighteenth century, or even before; it is therefore one individual of a population which extends over a vast area. In this country a number of plants appear to be hybrids, with broader, less glossy leaves; the type here described may be seen at Killerton, Devon, where it thrives in fullest exposure to the gales from Dartmoor, without suffering in any way.

The plant which has occurred in lists as *Rosa virginiana* 'Plena' has proved to be an old hybrid, correctly known as 'Rose d'Amour'; possibly a cross between *R. virginiana* and *R. carolina*. It is fully described , and its history given, in my book *Shrub Roses of Today*. It is trained on the west wall of Aberconway House, Wisley, and makes a remarkable display every July, the shapely wide flowers opening from scrolled buds.

It is often confused with the 'D'Orsay Rose'. The differences were pointed out in my notes in *The Rose Annual* for 1977, with pencil drawings.

Rosa virginiana

Although this rose has long been known in cultivation, having been discovered at Cherryfields, Maine, in the United States in 1867, its identity is uncertain. It was unhesitatingly classed as a variety of *Rosa carolina* in the 8th edition of Bean's *Trees and Shrubs Hardy in the British Isles,* but I think on rather slender evidence. It may well be a hybrid. Whatever it is, I find it a beautiful and satisfactory garden plant, and Parsons' picture is so well done and so appealing that I do not feel it should be omitted from this volume.

Like several of the American roses, when growing on its own roots it spreads freely by suckers; since it is a special individual it has usually been grown as a plant budded on a separate rootstock, in which case it is not likely to spread unless planted with the union well below ground. (In small gardens, of course, such a suckering habit is a disadvantage.) It will usually grow to about 90cm (3ft). The whole plant is inclined toward albinism, the stems being green and the foliage and other parts are all of a light green, assorting well with the lovely, wide, fragrant white flowers.

This rose is by no means alone in having been so long in cultivation under an assumed name. It has its parallel, too, in other species which were first seen and named from a double garden form rather than from the wild species which was not discovered perhaps until years later; examples in this book are *R. roxburghii* and *R. hemisphaerica.* This finding of the double or other large-flowered garden forms before the species is due to the fact that early collectors or observers from Europe tended to collect plants in gardens around the ports (particularly in China and Japan), long before the hinterland was explored.

Rosa virginiana Alba

The arching, interlacing twigs of glaucous or purplish tint, the straw-coloured prickles, the tiny leaves and the small, nodding, glittering scarlet heps mark this as a rose apart. In fact I rank it among the most ornamental of species, and although many of the flowers – on account of the interlacing branches – are borne inside the main structure of the bushes, they are revealed by the smallness of the foliage. As with *Rosa willmottiae* and *R. moyesii,* to both of which it is related, its display of heps is by far the longer lasting of its displays. The flowers are faintly scented.

The above refers to the plant we all know as *R. webbiana,* but it seems that perhaps it should be called *R. sertata,* which is a native of western China and was brought to France in 1897. *R. webbiana,* on the other hand, hails from Tibet, the Himalayas, Central Asia as far as Afghanistan, and was sent to Kew in 1879. Perhaps one day it will be agreed that they represent extreme forms of one species. They both make bushes of open habit, some 2.4m (8ft) high and wide; the plant I grow is apt to suffer in cold winters.

For those wanting a shrub with all the assets of *R. webbiana* but not the size, there is *R. webbiana microphylla,* often known as *R. nanothamnus.* This reaches about 1.2m (4ft) and is extremely attractive in fruit. It is found in similar areas to *R. webbiana.* Its small, bottle-shaped heps are of shining scarlet; the flowers pink.

97%

Rosa webbiana

A species of considerable vigour, trailing along the ground, with glossy, dark green foliage and creamy-white flowers, borne in large and small clusters from the axils of the leaves of the previous season, typical of the large section of Synstylae roses. They are remarkably sweetly scented and appear after midsummer, in fact as late as August in the south of England. It is quite hardy but has not received the attention it deserves in this country, though it is considered highly in the United States where its value as a ground-cover is esteemed for growing over graves, hence the name Memorial Rose.

It is a native of Japan and Korea and reached Kew from the United States in 1891; in France it had been named in 1871 as *Rosa luciae*, but subsequently was named *R. wichuraiana* (after Max Wichura of Breslau) in 1886. When there were so few rambling or climbing roses for our gardens, it was quickly adopted by the breeders and two distinct, colourful groups of ramblers were raised. The first group is typified by 'Dorothy Perkins' of 1901 from America and the second by 'Albéric Barbier' from France. The French hybrids were supposed to have been raised from a closely related rose, *R. luciae*, and this led me to conclude that this species caused the very considerable difference between the two groups when writing my *Climbing Roses, Old and New* in 1965. It later transpired that *R. wichuraiana* and *R. luciae* are to all intents and purposes synonymous; the difference in the two groups was therefore due to the fact that in America and in England parents were chosen from the older groups of Hybrid Perpetuals whereas the French had used Tea roses, hence the more glossy foliage, and larger flowers of cream, yellow and salmon or coppery colouring. These are moreover very fragrant; 'Dorothy Perkins' is not. However, 'Sanders' White' is sweetly fragrant and inherits some of *R. wichuraiana*'s late-flowering habit, still further exemplified by 'Crimson Shower'.

In common with the true *R. moschata*, the petals of *R. wichuraiana* tend to reflex.

Rosa wichuraiana

It is good to find that Miss Willmott, who did so much for roses, has this distinct species to her credit and, moreover, that the botanists have not had to change its name! It is usually wider than high, seldom ascending to more than 1.5m (5ft), but frequently twice as wide, its long arching branches glaucous when young and armed with pairs of short, sharp, forward-pointing prickles. The leaves have very small rounded leaflets, usually nine; these give the plant a pretty, lacy effect. The great spraying branches are decorated with plenty of flowers, usually of clear pink; some are darker, and I have seen some of lilac-pink. The small red heps are freely produced and lose their sepals early, a character which separates the species from various others. For early summer display it is scarcely surpassed.

It was discovered by E. H. Wilson when collecting for Messrs Veitch, from fairly arid valleys in Sichuan. It flowered first in Veitch's Coomb Wood nursery in 1907 and was named by them in honour of Miss Willmott. It was at a time when she would have been collecting historical facts about roses for her book and getting Alfred Parsons to paint them, in readiness for publication in 1910. It is sad that the Royal Horticultural Society's publications do not reveal that it was ever shown for an Award. She must have been proud of the naming for her of a new species in her favourite genus, and longed for it to be in good condition for one of the Shows.

Rosa willmottiae

In common with so many of the old roses which I have written about, this also has doubts and difficulties in regard to its nomenclature. At least, however, we know that it is attributed to the Reverend C. Wolley-Dod who gardened at Edge Hall, Cheshire; Parsons' painting is therefore of the authentic rose. But botanically it is not determined , being thought to be a hybrid of *Rosa villosa,* which is synonymous with *R. pomifera,* a native of central and southern Europe, Asia Minor and the Caucasus. It is established here and there in Britain as an escape from cultivation. 'Wolley-Dod' has been known as *R. villosa* 'Duplex' and *R. pomifera* 'Duplex', and a similar hybrid was depicted in 1799 by Miss Lawrance.

The two Latin names indicate the species' special characters: the greyish hairy leaves and the fruits – large, dark red, bristly and rounded, though not as large as those of an apple! Thus the species is yet another with two good seasons of beauty – June, when the single pink, slightly fragrant flowers blend so well with the downy leaves, and autumn, when the crimson fruits decorate the bushes, hanging in bunches.

Wolley-Dod picked out this rose because of its extra petals, making a more substantial and long-lasting flower, but the display of fruits is not so good as in the species. In both the petals are prettily crinkled. The great vigour of *R. villosa* imparts this quality to most roses grafted upon it. Dean Hole recalls a hedge "8-10ft high which is a sheet of bloom in May from the species itself and throughout the rest of the season with the Boursault, Noisette, Hybrid China and other Roses which are budded upon it." This is a thought for some of our public parks, perhaps; it could be quite a talking point in many circles of horticulture and a source of surprise to visitors.

101%

Rose 'Wolley-Dod'